Dressage Training and Competition Exercises for Beginners

Dressage Training and Competition Exercises for Beginners

Flatwork & collection schooling for horses

Elaine Heney

About the author and the letter Z

I live in Ireland. This dressage book is written using UK/Ireland English. I actually had no choice in this matter, as I spent my whole life learning how to spell like this in school in Ireland. I realise some dressage riders in the USA and beyond might be missing out on the letter Z. Here are some extra Z's just for you.

Zzzzzzzzzzzzzzzzzzzzzzz.

I hope they fulfill your Z expectations!

Enjoy the book, Elaine Heney, Ireland.

Horse books for adults

The Equine Listenology Guide
The Listenology Guide to Bitless Bridles
Ozzie, the Story of a Young Horse
Conversations with the Horse
Horse Anatomy Colouring Book

Horse books for kids

P is for Pony – The ABC Alphabet Book for kids 2+
Horse Care, Riding and Training for kids 6-11
Listenology for Kids age 8-14
Horse Puzzles, Games & Brain Teasers for kids 7-14

The Coral Cove Series for kids

The Riding School Connemara Pony
The Storm and the Connemara Pony
The Surprise Puppy and the Connemara Pony

The Connemara Adventure Series for kids

The Forgotten Horse
The Show Horse
The Mayfield Horse
The Stolen Horse
The Adventure Horse
The Lost Horse

Table of contents

"The greatest judge in this world is your horse. "

Elaine Heney

Introduction

Dressage is a great way to improve your riding skills and your horse's long term health. You can even go a step further and enjoy a day out at a local dressage competition and become part of a whole new community of like-minded equestrian friends.

Maybe you would like to work on your flatwork skills or improve your most recent dressage test results. Or maybe you're tired of seeing the words *'Needs more collection'* on your dressage test score sheet. You would love to be able to help your horse become more collected - without any gadgets, confusion or feeling like you're trying really hard but making no progress.

If you are thinking of attending your first show, and want to get prepared, we've got lots of tips and advice for you – from fun groundwork and riding exercises you can do at home with your horse to keep things interesting while you prepare, to tips for the warm up arena, advice on how to remember your test, and how to manage any nerves you might have on the day.

This dressage book is for all breeds of horses. It is designed for riders who are learning Introduction, Prelim and Novice tests, and working in walk, trot and canter. If you're more advanced but you've hit a roadblock, your horse feels stressed (or you do) or you know there are some fundamentals you need to fix - we've got lots of creative dressage exercises you can try.

Sometimes there is confusion that we must **'make'** the horse do dressage. We must make it trot, make it tuck its nose in or pull and push our way into a lateral movement.

That road doesn't go very far.

We end up with heavy horses, stressed riders who wonder why they are stuck at a level and can't seem to improve, and a general feeling that something is missing. Not to mention sore arms, legs like jelly and a confused horse. You can even end up thinking that either you or your horse isn't good enough. Or smart enough. Or you could do better if you had a different breed of horse. All of this is, thankfully, nonsense.

It's time to take the stress out of dressage!

Dressage doesn't have to mean 'stressage'. It can be a lot of fun. You can actually train a horse to be collected, light and responsive by communicating with its mind, instead of using excessive leg or hand pressure.

Feel like you're always pulling on your horse? Tired of your instructor telling you to use more leg? Does it just feel like hard work? **Perfect. You're in the right place.**

You don't need to do all of that to improve as a dressage rider. In fact, no rider should feel out of breath or be hot and bothered after a test. If you are, you're physically working too hard! Your horse is very smart, and if we can teach him the cues you need for the test, you won't have to work so hard physically yourself. So you can actually improve your dressage scores while doing a lot less in the saddle.

I realise dressage can seem like a black art. You get score sheets back saying *'more contact',* but you didn't get into dressage to pull more on your horse's mouth - and that seems to be what's wanted. Maybe you've been riding the same exercises for years and you're over it. Your horse is bored to death. You worry about what could go wrong on the day. Your friend got unexpectedly bucked off at her last dressage test. And let's not talk about the time you forgot the test entirely and had to retire...

A sneak peek of what lies ahead for you and your horse.

This book will give you the step-by-step fun exercises to build your confidence and knowledge, and help your horse become fitter, more relaxed and physically healthier. You can do this using a kind and no stress approach to dressage training.

Within this book you will find lots of practical groundwork, riding exercises and training ideas to help you improve your dressage test performance, and help your horse become more confident, relaxed and focused on you.

Plus as part of that process you will realise that you are creating lightness and softness in your horse and that riding dressage manoeuvres actually becomes much easier!

Your horse will be learning lots of cues that will improve the accuracy and scores in your dressage tests, plus I will also share the simple methods you can use to train your horse to become collected that have been used for hundreds of years – no arms of steel or massive leg muscles needed!

I've included a ton of tips on how best to prepare for your next dressage competition, including lots of checklists and exactly what you need to do to prepare in the week before your test – to maximise your dressage test scores.

Excited? So I am. So let's get started!

The origins of dressage

Dressage originated in ancient Greece and is described in 'On Horsemanship' and 'The Art of Horsemanship' written by the Greek commander, Xenophon. He wrote in great detail about how to train horses to be athletic and fit for battle and to work with them in harmony. It is a tradition that has echoed down the ages and developed into different schools and methods.

Currently there is a lot of controversy about how dressage should look and be ridden. Sometimes at competitions you can see that dressage can be done forcefully and in a way that is not the most beneficial way to ride a horse for the horse's health. Sometimes I look at the fixed hands, tension on the reins, over bent horses, and riders leaning way too far backwards, and ponder on how useless that style of riding would be to a working horse, maybe a war horse.

When a horse was being ridden in a battle, their riders would need them to be able to respond without a lot of direction from the hand. To respond quickly to very small cues. The riders would have had their hands busy with weapons and their focus would be on what was going on around them. So it makes sense that their horses needed to be well schooled and responsive, able to react to a shift in their rider's weight or a touch of their legs. To take it a step further and react to the riders thoughts.

A more modern comparison would be the working cow horse in the USA. Their rider is busy working from the saddle, they cannot micro-manage their horse's movements with strong hands and active legs. Their horses respond to cues from their body while their hands are occupied with a rope. How nice would it be to have our own horses able to respond to us in a light and responsive way, whether out for a ride in the countryside or in the competition arena? And no matter whether you live in the UK, Ireland, Australia, New Zealand, Canada, the USA or beyond?

My view is that horses should always be ridden in a way that supports them physically and mentally. We should look and feel like our horses' partners and be working for the benefit of the horse. **I feel that this is entirely possible, even when competing.**

Recently I attended an international dressage competition in Golega, Portugal. I watched many international dressage riders perform a very high level dressage test that included flying changes and piaffe.

It was fantastic to watch. But even though each horse and rider was competing in the same class, and so on the same level on paper, the style of each rider was completely different – ranging from very heavy handed and forceful riding, to riding that was effortless and considerate.

This competition is proof that you can be successful and rise up to international dressage level regardless of which approach you choose as a rider. We are going to focus on helping you succeed as a thoughtful rider with educated hands, and help you to use dressage both to succeed in competitions and to improve your horse's mental and physical health. Also, to have fun in the process!

Goals of dressage

Let's deal with the elephant in the room first. Let's look at what we don't want to do. It's said that a horse working at dressage should look like a 'happy athlete' and I agree 100% with that. Sadly, that is often not the case in modern times. Dressage can be horrifying to watch, over bent horses wearing severe bits and being ridden with hard hands. International top riders are rewarded for performances full of tension and force. In the warm-up rings at top level competitions horses can be seen subjected to 'Rollkur' with their heads forced into their chests and their pain showing in their eyes.

Unfortunately, many novice riders and even their trainers seek to emulate the professionals so much that they copy the bad examples.

My view is that dressage should be something that benefits my horse. I separate dressage from competition - doing well at dressage for me means having a happy, healthy and educated horse that can do some very useful movements that help to improve his posture and make him feel incredible to ride. Success in competition might be an added bonus. This is something that we all need to make our own decisions about.

If we go to a show and enter in dressage, what is the goal? It may be that the feedback from the judge was that you needed 'more contact'

– but you were perfectly happy with your light reins and could feel that your horse was collected and balanced.

The judge might mark you down because they felt that your medium trot was too slow – but you might be quietly celebrating the fact that your horse didn't take over and motor you out of the arena, as he did last time!

I say know yourself and your horse and celebrate what is important to you. Set your own competition goals, make improving your performance your number 1 goal, rather than comparing yourself too closely to the other riders. If you are confident in this it will help you to feel much less stressed in competition, and your relaxed state of mind will transmit to your horse.

I believe that dressage is not something to make us look good, or to get wins in competition with others. That is just a measure and by-product. For me dressage is a way to help your horse to feel great, improve their posture, and make it easier for them to carry the weight of a rider – doing the lovely natural movements that they produce when free in the paddock when they are under saddle.

For the rider it should feel easy and relaxed, their body will be in balance with their horse, their aids will be invisible and light and they will feel joy. There are no shortcuts to this, no magic gadgets to speed up the process, no forcing a horse to cooperate. It will be worth it.

Should you do dressage?

Dressage is like yoga for horses. It helps your horse become more flexible, more agile and improves their posture. We can all do dressage, and any horse can do dressage! This is because good dressage only asks the horse to carry out movements that they could do without a rider when they are playing in the field. A warmblood will look one way when they are working at dressage exercises, and they tend to be able to move in a way that is fashionable in dressage competitions at the moment. A cob will look a different shape but can be working beautifully in true collection with relaxation. An Arab or a Lusitano will look a bit different again. Learning the dressage movements in this book will take time, as we will be focusing on building your horses muscles slowly, and giving you and your horse time and patience to experiment, relax, and celebrate your progress.

If you want to keep yourself and your horse as fit and healthy as possible, dressage is a great addition to your training. You'll actually be able to feel your horse's fitness and agility improve, and notice that your aids are getting lighter and that your horse is getting much more responsive.

The benefits of dressage

Correct dressage training is designed to be healthy exercise for the horse. Done properly it helps develop mental and physical fitness in horse and rider. Teaching your horse new movements involves communication between you both and develops a great partnership.

Dressage gives purpose to working in the arena, which improves focus in the horse and rider. I promise you it's not all about trotting around in circles!

I like to break down each movement into tiny steps, and then I teach my horse each small step. This skill helps me become a better rider, and gives my horse lots of opportunities to get things right and feel proud of themselves.

The exercises and skills we learn from dressage will help us in other areas of our riding life. From negotiating obstacles on the trail to staying safely out of the way of a passing vehicle, the ability to ask our horses to respond quickly and accurately will help us on our journeys.

Tips for dressage success

You've decided to go for it! You're going to focus on improving your dressage skills, and how to train your horse to be your partner in the journey. So here are some practical tips to get started with. We need to take a look at your tack.

Tack for dressage training

Your horse needs to feel comfortable and relaxed in order to give their best in competition so it's up to us to make sure that their tack fits well and their body is as healthy as it can be.

The bridle

It's easy to get carried away looking at all the different bridles that are available to buy for our horses. As long as your bridle is in good condition and suits your horse's head that is all you need for the competition arena. So, tick that box - then concentrate on the most important thing, which of course is that we buy a bridle that fits well. Let's look at some key points:

The noseband

Nosebands should fit comfortably, giving the horse room to open their mouth properly and without putting pressure on or rubbing on their face. I would never use any noseband that forces my horse to keep their mouth shut. This will eliminate a lot of drop nosebands and flash nosebands that are commonly used by riders, but my choice is to allow my horse to breathe without restriction and move their mouth as much as they need to. If a horse is constantly opening their mouth or grinding their teeth when they're being ridden, they're trying to tell us something and it's up to us to find out what is causing the problem - rather than strapping their mouth shut so that they can't communicate with us anymore.

Sometimes people decide to use a noseband because they believe that it's necessary to stop their horse bolting off somewhere, or it helps them to improve their horse's brakes. What's going on here is that there is a training issue that is not being addressed or properly fixed. Instead there is a gadget being put on the horse to try and fix it, without doing the actual work needed to help the horse. If you actually take the time to fix the issue – which usually means going back a few steps and focusing on the foundations that were missed somewhere along the way – you'll end up with a WAY better horse than if you just try to fix the issue with a gadget.

You need to decide - are you a 'quick fix' type of rider, or someone who truly wants to improve and is willing to help your horse? Even if it means going back some steps to help your horse overcome the problem.

The Browband

The browband must be wide enough to give clearance at the base of the horse's ears. It's very common to see bridles where the browband and headpiece are too close to the ears. This results in the ears being pinched and rubbed and will be really uncomfortable for the horse. This is one of those things that once you are aware of it, you'll see it a lot. Many horses are ridden with browbands that are too close to their ears, but they stoically put up with it.

The Bit

The bit in your horse's mouth should be used for communication, not as a way to pull on the reins to make your horse tuck his nose in or lower his head. Your horses' mouth is incredibly sensitive (think of your own lips, teeth and gums!) so you need to find a bit that will fit them, which is often easier said than done.

When you are choosing a bit for your horse, ideally call in an independent bit fitter to make sure that you find the right one for them and you. If you can't do that, consider asking your equine dentist to visit to help. Every horse has a different mouth anatomy. So you benefit from having someone with experience to look inside your horse's mouth and let you know what they see.

People often seek advice on which bit to use with their horse from a local expert in a tack store or even the Internet! Every horse's mouth is different, so choosing a bit cannot be a one size fits all exercise. If you are fitting the bit yourself, make sure that you take into consideration the shape of your horse's mouth, the position of their teeth and the thickness of their tongue. When you think the bit is right, ride your horse to make sure that they feel truly comfortable with it. If you plan to take part in dressage competitions check the rules to make sure that your bit is 'dressage legal' for the level that you want to take part in.

Has your horse got sharp bars? Then a jointed bit won't work, when there is pressure on the reins the bit can press down on those sharp bars and will cause pain. This may lead to head tossing, bolting, bad brakes, etc.

Some horses have a tooth very close to where the bit lies in their mouth. Each time you use the reins, the bit actually hits this tooth. Imagine someone tapping your tooth with a metal bit for 45 minutes. Ouch. But again, the only way to see if this is an issue is to look inside your horse's mouth. I've heard it said that up to 10% of horses may have this problem, and any bit will never be suitable for them.

When you ride remember to think of your bit as a tool for communication, not control. Avoid pulling on the reins to try to force your horse into an 'outline'. The right head position for your horse will come from riding correctly and working on balance from behind. If you feel your horse getting strong so that you need to control them from the bit, take a break and think about what exercises you can use to work on their focus and flexion. Avoid riding in straight lines until your horse is listening to you and in control again.

If you have a horse that currently has any type of head or brakes issue – from leaning on the bit, avoiding the bit, getting their tongue over the bit, head tossing, head shaking, doesn't like being bridled - your homework is to see if you can identify any issues in your horse's mouth currently – from sharp teeth, or sharp bars to ulcers. An equine dentist or vet can help here - and then secondly to investigate if the bit you're using matches up with your horse's mouth anatomy.

The saddle

There are some pretty fancy saddles out there to spend your money on, but don't fall in love with saddles for their appearance or because somebody you know looks great riding in a particular make or model.

It can be a trap often fallen into. In Ireland, there is a popular make of jumping saddle that some of the top international riders use. The saddle is made in a northern country in Europe known for their warmblood horses. So this brand designs their saddle for the warmblood horse body type.

The only issue is that the up and coming Irish riders competing at local and national level who are riding Irish draught cross horses (not warmbloods) only want to buy this saddle brand, to be like the international riders they look up to. It's not uncommon in a yard for a lot of riders to spend many thousands of euros to buy this brand, ride in it, have it not fit the horse (even though the saddle sales person will say it fits fine) but then continue on riding in the saddle because it's their dream saddle, and they paid a lot of money for it.

It can be hard (or nearly impossible in my experience) to find a good independent saddle fitter, but ideally before buying any saddle that is what you need to do. However, there are some things you can do for yourself to check that your saddle is fitting well and is comfortable for your horse.

Before and after riding - back checkup:

Before you put your saddle on (at home or at a competition), run your hand over both sides of your horse's back and notice if there are any sensitive spots. Allow your horse to stand on a loose rein so he is able to move his feet if he needs to. If your horse reacts to the pressure from your hand by flinching or possibly even dipping his back suddenly, then consider getting your saddle checked before you ride again. Check your horse's back where the front of the saddle would lie. If your saddle is too narrow, your horse will have a sore back or shoulders here. Then check your horse's back when the cantle area of the saddle would sit. If your saddle is too long, it will put your weight on this weaker part of your horse's back, also likely to cause back pain for your horse.

After every ride take your saddle off and then, as above, run your hand over both sides of your horse's back to see if they react. Also look at the sweat pattern that may have developed under the saddle and whether any areas of your horse's fur are ruffled, which would indicate that the saddle is not sitting well. The saddle may be causing undue pressure or it may be moving around too much as you ride. If it's not the saddle that is the problem it's the pad that is underneath it. If your saddle pad is not fitting correctly with your saddle, it may move around when you ride or wrinkle up. This would also cause uneven sweat patterns and disturbed areas of fur on your horse's back. This would be very uncomfortable for your horse. Any of these problems will make your horse uncomfortable and make it difficult for them to move well when you're riding and to engage and lift their back.

Bear in mind that the lowest part of your horse's back should match up exactly to the lowest part of your saddle. This puts you seated in the strongest part of your horse's back, where they can best carry you, and in their centre of balance. You can check this by taking a photo of your horse from the side with and without the saddle. This will greatly improve your riding level, as you will now be sitting on the horse's balance point.

The channel created by the gullet of the saddle will need to be 3-4 fingers wide, to ensure that it does not touch the dorsal ligament system or spinal processes at all.

Shoulder movement

Make sure that the saddle doesn't interfere with the movement of your horse's shoulder blade as they move. It should sit 2-3 fingers behind the shoulder blade and its muscles.

No rider weight past the last rib

The saddle must not extend beyond the third lumbar vertebra or it will cause your horse pain and over time can affect their back long term. You can check this by locating your horse's last rib and drawing a straight line from it up to their spine. The saddle must not extend beyond that point and the weight of the rider should sit in front of that point.

Girth straps

The girth and billet straps should be pointing straight down and buckle up where they are supported by the breast bone. Put your hand flat behind your horse's elbow and make sure that they are sitting beside it.

Remember that the saddle needs to work for you as well as your horse. Get some photos and ideally a video of you in the saddle and riding. Look at your position to make sure that you are balanced and not tipping forward. If your instructor is always telling you to put your leg back, or adopt some type of position in the saddle, it's likely you have the wrong saddle. The correct saddle will naturally put you in the perfect riding position.

If you use large knee blocks pay attention to whether they are causing the lowest point of the saddle to move too far back. That would put you too far back, causing you to ride behind your horse's movement and risking causing them pain.

Gadgets

It's really common for tools to be recommended to deal with challenges riders are having with their horses. Side reins, bungee reins, flash nosebands, figure of 8 nosebands, tougher bits, harness around the rump... I do not use any of these things. If it straps it shut, holds it in place or forces a shape then it's not for me! There's always an answer that isn't forceful – it's up to us to find it. We become better riders and horse people when we do.

Look back at pictures from 50 years ago. You won't see horses with their mouths tied closed with these types of nosebands. It's just a fad.

Bitless, barefoot and treeless

The world of horsemanship is changing rapidly it seems. Just a few years ago treeless saddles were hardly heard of, but now they are very common and there are a wide variety to choose from. Bitless bridles were rare and often considered to be dangerous, but awareness is growing and they are becoming more common. It used to be the norm to shoe every young horse as they started to come into training for getting backed. Now owners are more likely to consider leaving those precious hooves unshod, and replacing shoeing with appropriate diet, environment and care. So where does that leave anyone who wants to compete in dressage?

Barefoot – does not seem to be a problem and probably won't even be noticed.

Treeless – a lot of competition riders who love treeless have identified such saddles that look 'treed' and are competing happily with judges none the wiser. However, appearances matter in dressage so it has been known for saddles (and other tack) that are less conventional in appearance to be marked down.

Bitless – forget it if you want to compete and be marked in a dressage competition. Sadly, at the time of writing bitless is not 'dressage legal'. If you want to take your bitless horse to the public dressage arena you will need to obtain permission from the organisers and strut your stuff without being marked.

Prepare yourself

We often spend a lot of time getting our horse ready to be ridden and compete and overlook the things that we can do to help ourselves. Looking after ourselves as a rider will not only help us to feel more comfortable and balanced in the saddle, it will also help our horse to carry us as easily as possible.

Find a good trainer

Lots of dressage instructors are wonderful. They love horses and they love their job. You can also get a lot of support from an instructor who just teaches good ridden techniques without a particular focus on dressage. Good riding is good riding and will help the horse whatever label is attached. These instructors get great satisfaction from seeing their students succeed.

However as with any profession, there can be a few bad eggs. Here are some warning signs to look out for, that may mean a change of instructor could be worth considering:

Force

They may be doing some very fancy and advanced moves on the horse, but when you look at how their hands are working and the shape of the horse's mouth you can tell that they are using excess pressure on the reins. They may be using the reins to force the horse's head into a position that they consider to be on the bit. Unfortunately, this gives you the clue that you are watching somebody who doesn't understand collection at all. They think it is about tucking the horse's head in mainly by pulling on the reins a lot – instead of realising that to collect a horse they need to teach the horse exercises, like shoulder out, that get the horse to step their hind legs under more deeply, and improve their posture.

Attitude

When they are teaching you, are they kind? Are they prepared to take the time to explain something again and differently if you don't understand what they're asking? Do they shout? During and after your lesson how do you feel? Do you feel happy and excited about what you've done or do you feel a bit demoralised, a bit down, possibly undermined?

Prepare to revisit the basics to fix issues instead of using gadgets.

When things aren't quite working between you and your horse - maybe you are struggling to work together in collection, maybe your horse is getting strong and running through your hands, or maybe they are very slow and reluctant to move. What is your instructor's reaction to this? They should be prepared to help you to go back to an earlier stage in your training to find out what's going wrong, and work on resolving it. If they reach for the nearest gadget, maybe to help you to keep your horse's head down, they look for a stronger bit to stop your horse pushing on your hands, or they instantly start to apply force to make your horse move more quickly – then they are taking short cuts and only addressing the symptom, not the cause.

Not seeing improvements

If you've been getting lessons from your instructor for a long time but have seen very little progress perhaps it's time to get someone else. With the right trainer you will see huge positive changes in just a few minutes!

So how do you find the right coach for you and your horse? Ideally get out and about and watch them teaching other people. See them ride. Ask for personal recommendations from friends and other riders who are doing what you aspire to. Even though training with your horse can be hard work, it should always be a positive experience for both you and your horse - so make sure you find the person who can help you to have that feeling.

Set out an arena

If you're lucky there will be an arena where you keep your horse that is set out with dressage markers and gives you a lovely surface and place to work in. However we're not all that lucky, sometimes we've only got a field to ride in. Make the best of what you've got. In a field you can still mark out an arena maybe with some electric tape (not electrified!) and some plastic posts. Invest in a set of dressage markers or make your own with some water containers filled up with water and some paint for the letters. Then you'll be set up and ready to go!

Arenas are usually either 20 x 40 or 20 x 60 metres. Competition arenas will usually be 20 x 60 metres. You'll have seen that they are marked out by letters, which help you to ride accurately and are used in dressage tests. Here's how to remember where to put them, starting with A at the top and going clockwise:

20 x 40 metre arena: All King Edward's Horses Carried Many Brave Fighters AKEHCMBF

Centre line: Doing Extra Good DEG

20 x 60 metre arena: All King Victor's Exceptionally Stunning Horses Can Manage Really Big Plastic Fences AKVESHCMRBPF

Centre line: Doing Lots Extra Is Good DLEIG

When a test says you have to change gait at a certain marker, the first step in a new gait should happen when the rider's body passes the letter/marker.

If you're working in an arena that you've created in the corner of a field there's going to come a time in the winter where you can't really use it anymore. Just remember that you can practise a lot of the things that you would do in an arena when you're out on a hack. Take advantage of a track that you're riding on to leg yield from side to side.

When you're opening a gate, make sure that your horse is soft in your hand and is backing up with correct flexion. If your horse's neck is tense, you can ask your horse to turn just their head to the left and right a few times (without moving their feet) so they can relax their neck. Then you're ready to ask for a soft and relaxed backup.

Use your forequarter and hindquarter yields to make gate opening easy. Practise square halts and backups when you reach a junction. Even though you are on a relaxed ride out, make sure that your horse is not pushing through your hands and be prepared to do some work to remedy that if they start. A responsive horse who is listening to you will be the one to keep you both safe. On top of that practising your dressage moves will become second nature for you and your horse.

Work on your posture without your horse

If you would like your horse to be more athletic and carry himself with good posture, then as his rider – if you really want to improve your riding skills - you really need to do the same too!

If you sit at a desk all day, it's likely you might end up with rounded shoulders, or a long list of other bad posture habits. Once we start developing these habits, we don't even notice we're doing them, And we do them everywhere. At work, walking around town, eating dinner, and riding our horses.

As riders we need good posture to be in balance in the saddle. Slouching, rounded shoulders, tipping forwards, or holding tension in our bodies is not going to help our horses.

It's worth considering joining a weekly yoga or Pilates session. The Alexander Technique taught for riders is brilliant as well. You can also find lots of free classes on YouTube that would greatly benefit your posture.

When to start dressage training

Young horses are often backed for riding at three years old. In some disciplines even younger! If you have a young horse you may come under pressure to do the same. I would never do that, and here's why:

I acknowledge that a horse's body is only physically mature at a minimum of 5.5 to 6 years of age depending on their gender, and that their back is the last part to develop. Many horses are still growing at age 7 and 8.

Horses all mature at the same rate. It is a myth that some breeds mature more quickly than others. Sometimes a particular breed, for example Thoroughbred racehorses, are brought up in a way that gives them a more physically mature appearance at a younger age. This does not change what is happening underneath, their skeleton is still developing at the same rate as their delicate looking, two year old Arabian counterpart.

For this reason, I would wait until a horse is three years old before starting any serious groundwork. Even then, I would still bear their immaturity in mind and work with them gently, not pushing them too hard. Keep the sessions short and fun. Use them to teach useful lessons for the future and build your horse's confidence. You can teach all sorts of dressage movements on the ground – like leg yield, shoulder out, backup and more), so when the time comes to try them in the saddle you've actually done most of the work already!

I do not ride two or three year old horses. Any type of gentle riding would only be when they are four years of age. Personally I start riding my horses when they are five years of age.

Dressage training movements and exercises

Let's start to think about some fairly simple exercises that you can do to prepare you and your horse for the dressage arena. Some of this might seem quite basic but if you get these foundations right, you will be putting the building blocks in place that will make it easier for you and your horse to learn the advanced work.

Remember, novice riders want to work on intermediate exercises. Intermediate riders want to work on advanced exercises. And advanced riders want to work on the foundation exercises. So think like an advanced rider.

Video yourself

Before we start here's a top tip - find a way to video yourself when you're working on the ground and riding. If you are squirming while reading this, I get it! But it's such a fast and effective way to improve your riding and posture in the saddle.

If you have a helpful friend who will stand by the side of your arena and record what you're doing, that's great! If not, there are various devices on the market, at varying prices, that you can attach to your phone and will follow you and your horse as you're working in the arena. While these are ideal, even if all you can do is mount your phone up on the arena fence or a tripod and capture some of your work it will still be helpful.

Sometimes you will look at the video of what you've done and be able to see areas where you can improve. You might also be surprised that what you actually did wasn't what you thought you were doing! You could also find that, even if you thought your training session wasn't going very well, you can see some good things that you and your horse did that you can build on.

Groundwork exercises – introduction

Now we will look at some simple groundwork exercises that are designed to develop your horse's balance, straightness, suppleness and flexion. It doesn't matter what size or breed of horse you have; these exercises will help them all. Even if they're not going to compete, groundwork done correctly can improve the health of all horses. Working in relaxation with true collection will help horses to stay physically and mentally healthy as they grow older. We are always training our horses for the long term.

Maybe you can gain some inspiration by watching videos of the Haute Ecole groundwork done by the riders at the Spanish Riding School in Vienna. They teach movements right up to levade, piaffe and passage from the ground!

I use a rope halter with a 12 foot, clip-less, line for groundwork with my horses and I really recommend that you do the same. I also use a flag on a lightweight stick, to gently ask for my horse's attention and focus and direct them. The reason I use a flag is because I never want to pull on my horse. Pulling creates braces and tension.

Instead if I ask my horse to move by lifting the lead rope, and there is no movement, instead of pulling on the lead rope, I just lift the flag instead. So I am keeping the lightness in my horse, and avoiding problems down the road. I try to never pull on my horse – whether it's in groundwork or in riding. Pulling is a big habit many horse people have, but when you stop pulling on your horse, you'll see a huge positive change in all aspects of groundwork and riding.

A note about rope halters - they don't break.

Conventional halters have break points built in that should break if under extreme pressure. This is not the case with rope halters. So never turn a horse out, or leave them in a stable, or travel them in a horse box or trailer, wearing a rope halter. If you tie up your horse in a rope halter, tie to something that will break quite easily if they get scared. Never leave a horse alone when they are wearing a rope halter. A lot of people travel their horses in them, but I choose not to and use a conventional halter with break points for that.

If your horse is not used to you using a flag, make sure you work gently with them before starting the exercises, to ensure that they are not afraid of it. They should not be so desensitised that they ignore it, but they should respond to it in a relaxed way and without being frightened.

In the next section you'll discover the basics of groundwork and I hope you'll have fun trying the exercises out. They are a great way to add fun and variety into your training sessions with your horse.

Use these exercises as a starting point and then, when you and your horse are confident with them, think about how you can keep life interesting by mixing them up. These are the exercises I use and highly recommend.

Groundwork exercises – halt and backup

These two are so important. It's not just about having our horse come to a halt any old way. We are looking for our horse to halt immediately when we ask them to. We would like our horses to halt by using their hindquarters, instead of stopping by putting extra weight on their forequarters. We will be looking for them to feel balanced and soft in the hand. When they stop, they will actually be thinking backwards.

They will not be trying to push through the halter to start moving forward before we ask. The halt and the backup, used together, are powerful tools for developing a balanced and collected horse who is able to shift their weight onto their hind end easily.

Backup

Backup is one of the most important keys to collection. If your horse doesn't back up very well, or keeps their weight on their forequarters while they back up, you're going to struggle to collect your horse.

Recently I was watching an FEI dressage competition at Madrid Horse Week in Spain. During the test they had to halt at C and take a few steps backwards. The steps should have been in diagonal pairs and performed smoothly, without any stops and starts. A lot of these international dressage horses struggled with this, as to perform it correctly the horses needed to be truly collected, not pushing forwards onto the bit, and relaxed. Only a few rode this movement correctly.

When your horse backs up, we are looking for their legs to move in diagonal pairs. When your horse is backing up correctly, they will be carrying more weight on their hindquarters (perfect to improve collection and self-carriage), and the flexion of the hind legs, back joint and lumbosacral joint will be increased. This is all exactly what we want our horses' bodies to do, to help them become more collected and greatly improve their posture, engage their abdominal muscles and develop back mobility.

To back up easily, your horse needs to feel relaxed and not carry a lot of tension in their body or neck.

Hold the knot under the halter with **your thumb pointed downwards.**

Step 1: With the halter on your horse, stand beside him, put your hand on the knot where the lead line attaches to the halter and ask your horse to move his head gently from side to side. Do this with your thumb pointing downwards. The goal is for this movement to

feel really easy and smooth. But your horse at the beginning may be tense, and brace against your hand, not wanting to turn his head a little left and right. So instead of looking for the perfect end result, we would just like a tiny improvement. One split second when you notice your horse relaxing their neck a fraction. Then take your hand off the halter and have a rest. Let them think about it. In doing this we are breaking down a task into lots of tiny little steps. Repeat again, and look for a tiny improvement, then release. Work on these for 2-3 minutes over a few days, until you can feel that the tension in your horse's neck has released and this feels much easier to do.

The goal here is we would like your horse to relax and soften his neck, as your fingers gently touch the halter knot. We need a relaxed horse in order to back up correctly.

Step 2: When you put your hand on the halter knot (thumb down) and it's easy to move your horse's head a little right and left, you should notice your horse is also happy to lower their head a little when you ask gently. Now you're ready to ask for backup. If you're not at this stage, go back to step 1.

Close your fingers around the knot. Very gently think backwards, and move your hand a tiny bit backwards. You are looking for your horse to only shift their weight back a fraction. We're not looking for an actual step yet! Just a backwards thought. Remember, baby steps. You can also add a vocal cue 'back' when you do this. This is handy as you can also use it later when your horse is loose and you want them to step backwards!

When you get the thought of 'back' from your horse, release, take a break. Your horse might yawn, or lick or chew. This is all great. They're thinking about it. Thinking time when you're training is really important.

Then ask again. For the first day, just aim for a weight change backwards - and release. I'd only do this for 1-2 minutes maximum. Over the next few days you can work up to one step or even maybe two or three steps back. Remember, the goal is not to backup. The goal is to first have a relaxed horse without unwanted tension and braces, and for the horse to understand the cue.

Halt:

The secret to a really good halt is to train your horse to go backwards for two or three steps after they halt. This way, both on the ground and when you ride, when you ask your horse to halt, they are actually thinking backwards. Then you get a wonderful halt with the horse using their hindquarters. You can take the backward steps out when your horse really gets this, but if your halt starts to become unbalanced put them back for a while.

Walk, halt, then backup

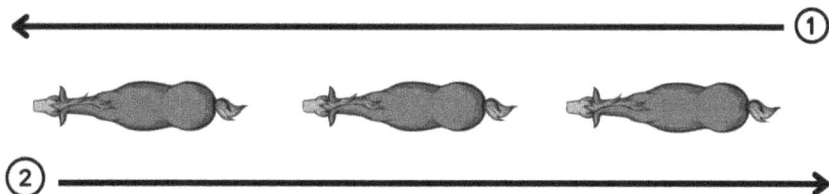

Try this exercise to practise your halt and backup on-line:

Hold your lead rope in the hand closest to your horse, allowing about 3 ft of rope between you. Have your flag in your outside hand. Stand by your horse's shoulder and stay there for the exercise. Look straight ahead of you, raise your energy, and step forward. If your horse doesn't immediately walk forward with you, reach behind you with your outside hand to shake the flag to encourage your horse forward.

If at any time your horse starts to turn towards you, bring your flag forward and hold it out ahead of you to encourage them to straighten up. If they start to pull away a little just gently put a feel on the rope and release it, while asking them to move forward with the flag.

Ask for the halt by first of all slowing your steps. Have your flag by your side as you stop. If your horse carries on going forward, immediately lift your flag and put it out in front of your horse to explain that they need to stop.

If your horse has understood the backup training, at this stage you should be able to ask them to backup straight for a few steps. Stay positioned beside their shoulder, lift your hand a little and put a backward feel in the rope. If they need a bit of help raise your flag in front of them to explain. Just get two or three good steps and stop. Let them think.

When your horse understands what you want in this exercise you will be able to stop more quickly and soon be able to stop without first slowing your steps, and your horse will too! You will also be able to ask for more steps of backup. Try counting your forward and backup steps and gradually increase them.

Potential pitfalls:

The horse is still thinking 'forward' after halting. You will feel this in the form of pressure in your hand. They might be leaning forward, or they might lift a front hoof and actually step forward. You need to be aware of this and gently and consistently correct it. If your horse is still pushing forward, ask for a step or two more of backup. Repeat as required.

In the backup your horse might tense and hollow their neck during the movement. Take a mental step back and concentrate on asking your horse simply for soft flexion – the ability to flex their neck without over-bending - and ask them to drop their head a little. Then return to asking for a backup, just one step at a time, while maintaining this feel and flexion.

Groundwork exercises – yields

Before we can even think about lateral work, such as shoulder in or leg yield, we need to have the ability to have our horse move their hindquarters or forequarters independently, first when standing still, then when moving forward. I always teach this first on the ground.

Forequarter yield

We would like our horse to move their front two legs 1 step to the side. Their two hind legs stay in the same place.

Ask your horse to **move his two front legs** 1 step to the side

I'll explain two ways of doing this.

Method 1: Stand in front of your horse, lift your rope and gently take it out to the side. This will turn your horse's head in the same direction, and if you maintain that feel, they will take one step out to the side. If they don't understand at first, you might find it helpful to swing the free end of the rope, or raise your flag, in the direction of the shoulder that needs to move over. If they take more than one step, or start to follow with their hind legs, it means that you can probably ask with even less of a feel on the rope or 'energy'. Experiment to see how little it takes.

Method 2: Think about how shifting your horse's balance can help them to move just one front hoof. In this method you will be aiming to ask first for a backup, then aiming to ask for the hoof nearest to you to take one step towards you just as it starts to leave the ground.

Stand by your horse's shoulder. Hold your rope in the hand furthest from your horse. Take your hand across your body so that it will be close to your horse, lift the rope and ask your horse to backup. Make sure that you move with them. Let them take one step back, then as the hoof nearest to you starts to leave the ground again, move your hand away from your horse's body so that it asks them to flex their head towards you a little bit. If you time it right, their hoof will follow. Make sure that you also step to the side, to allow your horse to move over. Then stop and let your horse think. The aim is to have just that one step to the side, with the hind hooves staying still.

When your horse finds this easy on both sides you can build on this. The sequence would be one step back up, one step to the side, one step back up, another to the side and so on. But don't overdo it, one step at a time and try to quit when your horse is doing well.

Move the shoulder out on a circle

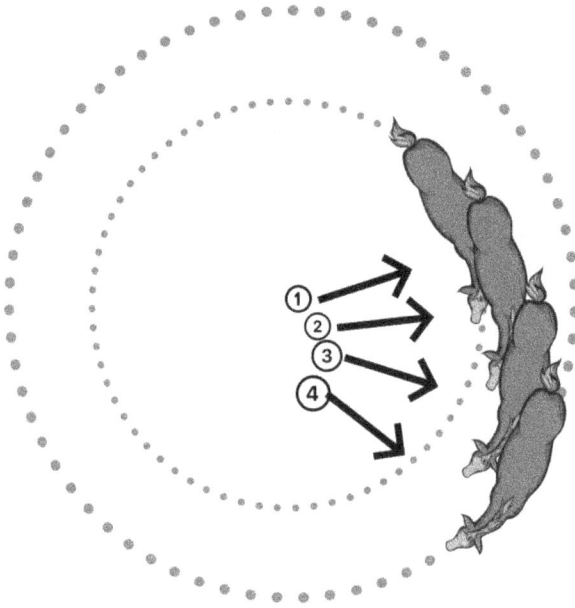

Ask your horse to **move his shoulders** away from you on a circle, and make a bigger circle.

Once you and your horse understand how to move their shoulders, ask your horse to go forward and ask for the yields as you walk together side by side. You can touch their shoulder to ask your horse to move it away from you. Touch their barrel where your leg would sit when riding to ask them to step sideways. Reach back with your flag to ask their hindquarters to move over. I suggest that rather than asking your horse to give several steps of a yield, you reward the slightest try, even if it's just a tiny step, by allowing them to immediately go straight again. This will help them to understand that they are doing what you want, and you can build up the number of steps gradually.

Then build on this by working on a circle. Start by walking beside your horse's shoulder in a straight line. Have your lead rope in the hand furthest from your horse, and your flag in your inside hand. Make sure that you have some slack in the rope. Then, ask your horse to tip their head slightly towards you, while moving the flag towards their shoulder to ask it to yield over. Don't stand still as if you were lunging, turn towards and move with your horse, staying in line with their shoulder. As you gradually let the rope go longer, and ask for your horse to move their shoulder over, your circle will get bigger. Make sure that you maintain that soft bend towards you, if you start to lose it, direct your flag towards your horse's barrel to ask for it back.

Hindquarter yield

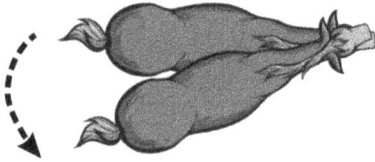

Ask your horse to **move his two hind legs** 1 step to the side

Leg yields are valuable suppling and relaxing exercises for the horse. They help young and inexperienced horses to become more balanced. Hindquarter yields strengthen the horse's hind end and encourage them to take more weight on to their hindquarters. This shift of balance to the hind end is, as I've mentioned before, the foundation of true self carriage.

Here are two ways to work on hindquarter yields:

The most simple way to start is by working quite close to your horse on the ground. Stand by your horse's shoulder, with your lead rope in the hand closest to their head. Face slightly towards their hind end. Ask them to flex their neck and head softly towards you, without starting to move their legs. If they do start to take a step, take your time, move with them until they stop, then pause and ask again, ask for less so that they learn that you only want them to flex their neck without moving.

When your horse is flexed softly towards you, use your free hand to touch them on the side, where your leg would be when riding, and use gentle pressure to ask them to step over. You are looking for both of their hind legs to move, but for their front legs to stay still. You can also try this by having your flag in your free hand, facing your horse and pointing it towards their hindquarters to ask them to move. As always, do this in both directions.

The benefit of having your horse able to yield their hindquarters at a cue from the stick will transfer to when you are in the saddle. If you need your horse to move their hindquarters, and maybe they don't understand at first, you will be able to point the flag towards their hindquarters to explain.

Ask the inside hind to step under on a circle

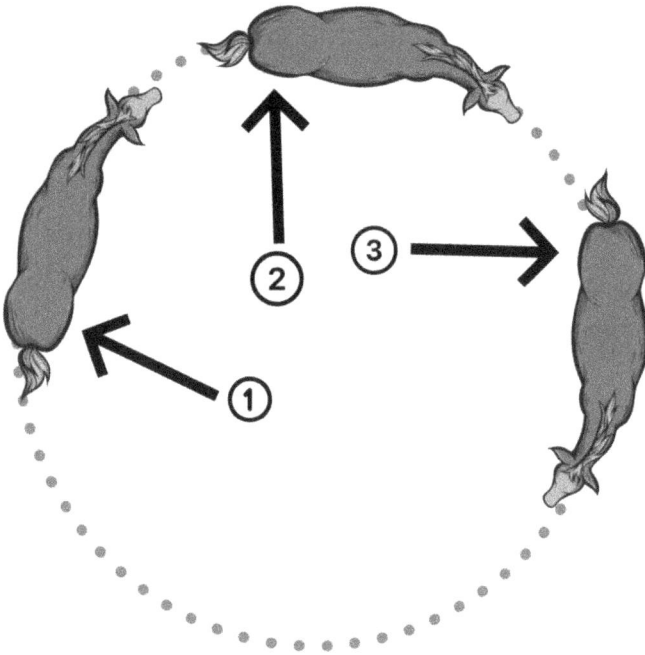

Ask your horse to step his **inside hind foot** more deeply underneath his body. This creates more bend in his body.

Another way to practise yielding the hindquarters is to ask when your horse is moving on a circle. Ask your horse to move out around you on a circle, as described above. Don't send your horse too far away from you at first, move with them so that they are not restricted, but have about 2 metres of rope between you. Have your flag in your free hand. Make sure that your horse maintains the bend around you. Watch their hind hooves lifting up and hitting the ground. You are going to point your flag towards your horse's inside hind hoof to ask for it to move away from you. It will be much easier for your horse to do this if you time your 'ask' as the inside hoof is leaving the ground. Don't ask for lots of steps, one is fine at first, then let your horse return to the simple circle. As you and your horse get to understand this exercise you will be able to increase the size of your circle and work further apart.

Potential pitfalls:

The most common challenges I see when horses are working on hindquarter and forequarter yields are the horses either stopping, going too fast or turning towards their handler.

These issues are really all about position. You need to be moving in line with your horse's shoulder. If you start to get a bit ahead of your horse, maybe even if you are only walking in line with their neck instead of the shoulder, the horse will feel their movement blocked and slow down or stop.

If you fall too far behind your horse it is very likely that they will flex their neck a bit more and start to turn towards you. Think of there being a 'drive line' on your horse's barrel, roughly where the girth would sit. It's a good place to point your flag behind if you want to send your horse forward when working your horse on a circle, effectively driving from behind the line. However, if you fall back behind that line, you will effectively start to draw them towards you.

Groundwork exercises – walk in hand

Where are you in relation to your horse's body when you are walking together? In front? By their head or shoulder? Or do you not really pay much attention to this at all? There are varying opinions on this, but personally I like to walk by their shoulder. This puts me 'in reach' of their head or hind end. I teach my horses to give me space when we are together, and to respond when I ask them to move their shoulder away from me.

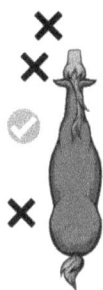

Walk beside your horse's shoulder using a loose lead rope. Don't walk in front of your horse and pull him along behind.

Hold your lead rope in the hand closest to your horse, allowing about 3 ft of rope between you. Have your flag in your outside hand. Stand by your horse's shoulder and stay there for the exercise. Look straight ahead of you, raise your energy, and step forward. If your horse doesn't immediately walk forward with you, reach behind you with your outside hand to shake the flag to encourage your horse forward.

When you want to halt with your horse, slow your feet and stop. If they don't understand, be ready to put your flag out in front of them and shake it to help them.

A lot of people only think about walking together with their horse and leading correctly when they are working in the arena. My advice is to follow these good habits every time you are with your horse.

The more consistent you are with your horse the easier they will find it to understand what you want and do it. They won't understand why they are asked to go, walk and halt nicely sometimes, but at other times they can wander about at the end of the rope anyhow. They will understand if you ask them to do the same thing, with the same cues, every time you are leading together.

So, practise walking with energy and purpose every time you have your horse in the halter and rope. Make sure that they walk forward immediately when you do, and stop neatly when you do. Be aware if they don't stop when you ask and use the backup to correct that. You may need to carry your flag every time you are leading your horse for a while, but that is just a training phase.

Potential pitfalls:

You can probably add a lot of potential leading horse pitfalls to this! I'll just talk about the two that first came to me. That is – horses getting ahead of the human and crossing in front of them, and horses using their outside shoulder to pull away from their human. Often to grass or another tasty treat.

If your horse is pushing on you and starting to turn towards you and cross over your path – lift your flag up and out in front of them to create a visual barrier to discourage them. Flap the flag if you need to, to get their attention. You may find that you lose the argument at first and they manage to cross in front and start to go around you. If that happens don't get into a fight, bring them right around so that they are facing in the original direction and think ahead to put your flag out to the side and in front to stop them circling, ask them to go straight.

If you feel your horse start to pull away from you, try to catch that thought as soon as it starts to happen! Think about the fact that if your horse's hind end is moving away from you, their head will have to come around towards you. So reach back with your flag and ask the hindquarters to move over. This may be all it takes, but if your horse is a bit more determined be prepared to step back, turn towards their hindquarters, and look at them while directing your horse to move over.

A word of caution here. If your horse is very bothered don't make yourself vulnerable by getting hard with your flag, and being too close to the back end. I think the potential consequences of that are obvious, and the first priority is to stay safe.

Groundwork exercises – different speeds

So you've tried some groundwork and you and your horse seem to understand each other pretty well. Now it's time to work on upward and downward transitions of gait. We can't run as fast as horses, so you will want to work in circles.

Avoid lunging

My suggestion is to avoid conventional and repetitive lunging, instead move with your horse, even when they are out at the end of the line, and think about travelling around the arena rather than circling in one place.

Lunging where you just stand in the middle of the circle can cause a few problems that are better avoided. These include bad posture - the horses tend to move around looking to the outside of the circle and with the wrong (unbalanced) bend. Why teach your horse to move in an unbalanced way when it is so easy, as described earlier, to teach a way that is more beneficial for them? The repeated circling can also be a strain on the horse's joints.

Lunging will both physically tire horses out and get them fitter. So if you had a horse you lunged because you were afraid they'd bolt off, they will now still be the same horse that might bolt off, but now they can bolt faster as they are fitter. Instead we need to find out why they are bolting. Too much energy? Maybe they need less food and more turnout. Running to get away from pain? Check their back and teeth and talk to your vet. Every behaviour has a cause.

I think we need to question whether lunging is an interesting and positive experience for the horses. They need to be engaging with us, not drilled round in repetitive circles. As humans we need to have a second-by-second conversation with our horse, rather than standing in the middle doing very little while our horse mindlessly runs around us.

Changing Speed Exercise

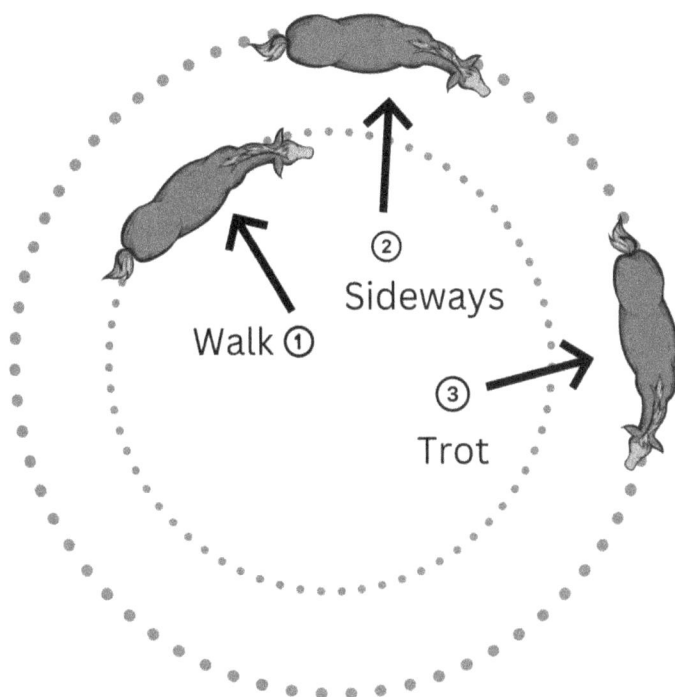

Ask your horse to **move his shoulders** away from you on a circle, and make a bigger circle. Then **ask for trot**.

Walk with your horse on a straight line, aiming to stay in line with their shoulder. Start by walking quite close beside your horse's shoulder. Ask for a little neck flexion towards you (so they are looking at you a little) and push their shoulder away from you so that they yield out and start to move on a circle. Think about walking towards your horse's shoulder, and your horse moving his two front legs sideways away from you.

Stay walking with them in line with the shoulder, even though the distance is getting bigger. As your horse starts to work further away you will probably find it useful to have your flag in your free hand.

To ask for a transition up to trot, lift your rope hand slightly and visualise your horse making that transition. If you need to, lift your flag so that it points just behind their backside to encourage more forward. As soon as your horse trots, relax, let out a deep breath and visualise a walk. If your horse does not understand, lift your flag up so that it points out ahead of them, shake it gently if need be to encourage them to slow down. Watch for your horse to be soft in the neck, with their head tilted slightly towards you and giving the impression of a curve around you through their body.

Gradually increase steps in trot until your horse is trotting happily round and returns to walk, then halt, when you ask. Then you are ready to progress to canter in exactly the same way.

Potential pitfalls

Your horse might keep turning in towards you. You might have fallen behind the drive line (as above) and be inadvertently drawing them towards you. The answer is to work on your position and stay aware of it. You might also be able to gently lift your flag up between you and your horse's neck/head to encourage them to stay out on the circle.

Here's another thing that can draw your horse's head in towards you – too much hand when you ask them to move on or make a transition. You will often see people lifting their rope hand right out to the side in the direction their horse is going, with the aim of leading their head or encouraging more speed. This puts pressure on the horse's head, however subtle, and is effectively pulling the horse towards them. Instead just lift your hand, maybe point in the direction you want with your finger (more for your benefit than your horse!) and send them on by pointing your flag at their barrel.

Ideally you can do this by not moving your hand, just by pointing your finger! Small cues are a wonderful product of great training and understanding between you and your horse.

The obvious thing that goes wrong a lot with changes of gait on-line is that horses get a bit carried away and go too fast. If that happens to you, take one of those mental steps back – think in terms of just one step of what you want. Ask for the trot, just one step, then immediately relax down to walk. Your horse will start to look for slowing down instead of rushing off, and you can build up the trot, and then the canter, just one step at a time.

If your horse is really determined to rush, and motoring around you on the rope, here's another idea to try. Move your hands on your rope and walk backward until you are holding it quite near the end. Walk in a big arc away from your horse, curving round so that you aim to pass behind them at a safe distance from their hind end. Keep walking that circle. Your horse will need to turn their head around to follow you. When you feel their attention shift and them slowing down you can offer them the chance to stop. You can practise this when they are not running away of course, after you've done it a few times your horse should start to look more to you, anticipating you asking them to follow.

Groundwork exercise – shoulder out

While most people may have heard of the exercise shoulder in, in fact the very first lateral exercise I recommend you do with your horse is called shoulder out.

Shoulder out is an exercise I like to teach first on the ground and then once the horse and the human understand it, we can repeat it in the saddle.

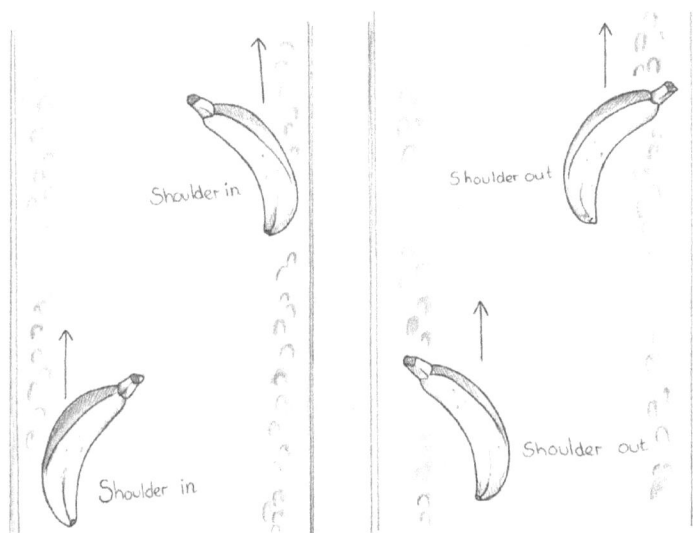

Imagine the smaller end of the banana is the horse's head.

You will be asking your horse's body to bend in a similar way to how this banana is bending!

We are looking for a gentle bend through your horse's whole body - not just in the neck.

Shoulder in and shoulder out are very similar. In shoulder out the horse's head is pointing towards the fence line, with their hindquarters more towards the inside of the arena. During shoulder in the horse's head is pointing towards the inside of the arena, with their hindquarters close to the fence line.

I have some good news for you! You DO NOT need a dressage arena to do this! You can do this on trail rides, along a fence line, on the ground - anywhere you want.

How to teach shoulder out:

Just to be on the safe side, make sure that your horse is comfortable with you touching their hindquarters all over and moving close to their back end. Check that your horse has remembered their lessons on moving their hindquarters by asking them to move just one step, by touching their ribcage where your foot would be if you were riding.

You are going to work along the fence line of your arena or exercise paddock. Walk along the fence at your horse's shoulder, with you between them and the fence. Look ahead and make sure that you are both facing forward. Do this a few times in both directions.

Walk along the fence line again, this time allowing your horse to drift ahead of you a little as you go. There should be plenty of room to do this when you are using a 12ft line. As your horse starts to get ahead, they will naturally start to move sideways, looking out of the arena. You will be walking towards their ribs, which will help the sideways movement.

Build this up slowly. Just get one step of lateral movement then ask your horse to go straight. If you ask for too much too soon your horse is likely to get confused.

Potential Pitfalls

I think the most common setback I see when people are learning this exercise is their horse stopping when they start to bend, rather than continuing to move forward. This is all about impulsion – the horse and human need to be stepping out smartly together, looking forward and with a rhythm about their walk. Bear this in mind if things start to grind to a halt!

Just by doing this shoulder out exercise you will see a lot of benefits:

- It will improve your horse's balance.
- It will encourage your horse to transfer weight from forequarters to hindquarters.
- It will help your horse become more athletic.
- It will improve your horse's physical posture.

- It is the beginning of collection (which is the healthiest way for a horse to carry the weight of a rider).
- It will help the horse to be able to move and turn with more agility and flexibility.
- When you ride your horse will feel lighter and more responsive to smaller cues.

Now, you might be thinking, do you need some sort of fancy dressage horse to do this? The answer is no. Any horse can do this! From quarter horses and Arabs to thoroughbreds, paints and cobs.

Groundwork exercises – get outside

This is a simple bit of advice – learn your exercises in a safe space like an arena or paddock. Then get out and about and have some fun together. Riding is great, but so is walking out with your horse. It builds your relationship. It gives you opportunities to use the movements you've learned in a natural environment using trees and other landmarks as markers. It gives you and your horse some down time together. It also helps to keep the rider fit!

Why groundwork?

You might be wondering why I've talked about working with horses on the ground when dressage is a ridden discipline. Some dressage trainers don't teach groundwork exercises and you are always riding during their lessons.

It is my belief that every horse will benefit from good groundwork. It's a fun way to try something different and it can be easier to learn new moves on the ground, where you can see what your horse's four legs are doing. Plus as you are not riding, you've got less to think about, and sometimes a greater chance of success.

We want to make our lessons as simple as possible for your horse to understand, but we also want to make it simple for us to succeed in dressage! This starts right at the beginning of training.

If you and your horse can do beautiful transitions, sideways, halts and backups and more on the ground, think how much easier they will all be when you ride the same manoeuvres.

Groundwork is an interesting and varied way to work on horses' balance and muscle development. Groundwork will also help them to learn to respond to light cues from their human, giving a foundation that translates into ridden work. It also gives us, the humans, the skills to feel secure with our horses on the ground, and to feel confident that we can ask them to listen and respond to us when we have a rope in our hands.

If things feel a bit stressful, as they might at a large competition venue, horses and riders can often get some relaxation and focus by working together doing some thoughtful groundwork exercises to calm down and connect to each other, before the rider gets on board.

Riding exercises – introduction

Everything that we and our horse learned together on the ground has prepared us for our ridden work. Everything we practise when we're riding prepares us for our next competition.

Everyone who competes in dressage will know how to ride these movements. Here's a thing though – not everyone will understand the difference between riding them in a forceful and rigid way, and riding them in a true partnership.

Why not go out and watch some dressage competitions as part of your preparation for taking part?

And why not go further! Maybe you can find an international FEI event to attend? That's a wonderful way to get the bigger picture of the path you're on when you start doing dressage tests.

Don't look too hard at the riders at first – instead look at their horses. Do they look relaxed? Are their eyes soft? Are they wearing tack that looks comfortable, with a bridle that isn't clamping their mouth shut? Is their bit stable in their mouth or being dragged backwards and forwards by the reins? Is their neck softly bent at the poll, with the poll at the highest point? Or is the poll lower than the highest bend in their neck (often referred to as over-bent).

When you've decided which horses look as happy as you'd like your horse to be – then look at their riders. Learn from watching people who are doing what you want to do, and who look happy and relaxed doing it. They might not be the people with a trainer leaning on the rail giving them instructions. They might not have the smartest looking horse, or the most expensive tack, or be wearing the latest trendy clothing. They will be the people who put their horses first.

Remember this when you're riding at home. Concentrate on having your horse as happy as you can. Make sure you don't 'drill' the work. Learn when to quit – if you've just felt your horse do the most perfect shoulder out you've ever experienced what do you do? Do it again, or jump off, give your horse a lovely rub and turn them back out in their field to chill?

Also be creative about how you use the movements and exercises available. You will use them in a disciplined way to learn your tests, but also make sure to mix things up, be creative, make up your own tests. Enjoy the learning.

Don't over bend your horse.

One dressage training method that you need to avoid at all costs is to ride in a way that tucks the horse's head into his chest, in hyperflexion. It's seen in the warm up area and you can't miss it. This is extremely bad for a horse's health, as it's stressing all the wrong parts of their body, and is likely over time to cause physical damage. An extreme version of this is seen in trainers and riders who use Rollkur, where the horse's neck is hyper flexed to bring their head right down to their chest, and their rider then works their head from side to side. Sadly, in modern dressage the resulting performance in the dressage arena has been known to win at the highest level. Fortunately, the tide seems to be turning against such abusive training methods. The FEI banned Rollkur in the warm up arena in 2010, although it's known to still be practised by some high-level riders.

While I understand the goal is for the horse to look collected – we must actually COLLECT the whole horse's body (which starts with exercises using the hindquarters) and just pulling your horse's head in, to make a 'shape' just isn't the same thing. If your trainer is teaching you to ride your horse with its head tucked into its chest, they do not understand collection, are harming your horse's posture and health and I would suggest finding a better and more educated trainer to train with.

When beginner dressage goes wrong

Recently I was at a local dressage competition in the UK. I met a lovely guy who had started riding later in life, and who had done a few low level dressage competitions. He absolutely loved his horse. I watched him ride, and could not believe my eyes as I watched him ride his dressage test, with arms of steel and the horse over bent to the point that the horse's chin touched his chest for 99% of the test. It was horrendous. The stewards should have stopped it – but they didn't. If someone had videoed it and put it on Facebook, there would have been war. But this guy had absolutely no idea of what he was doing to his horse. He had paid a lot of money to a trainer to teach him, and his trainer had told him to ride like this. To ride with something that looked very similar to Rollkur. He had the right horse and the right goals, but the wrong trainer.

Collection – what it is and isn't

You will hear a lot of talk about collection. On your dressage test score sheet you may have seen the words *'more collection needed'*.

People will discuss a horse being on the bit, taking up a contact and working in an 'outline'. It's very common for riders and trainers to be looking for a horse to be in a particular shape, with their head in a certain position, to show that they are collected.

There are two major schools of thought on how to achieve this:

School 1: Pull a lot on the reins to hold the head down and use a lot of leg pressure. This does not collect the horse, and shows the trainer has really no understanding of what collection actually is. This method also is very damaging for your horse's body.

School 2: Understanding that to collect your horse you do not pull on the reins or use a lot of leg. Instead, you put in the time to teach your horse new groundwork and ridden exercises that positively change your horse's posture.

The truth about collection is that it is not making a horse move in a particular shape, and it is all about balance.

Collection is simply a shift of weight from the forequarters to the hindquarters.

Collection helps the horse to carry the rider's weight in a way that is more balanced and athletic.

The aim is to have them working in true self-carriage without the need for the rider to physically hold them with their hands or legs to maintain that.

Horses have no problem working in true self-carriage when they are playing in the field, but they need help to do the same when they are carrying a rider's weight.

When the horse's balance shifts more to the hindquarters, a few things happen.

- One or both hind legs step under their body more deeply.
- The angle of their pelvis changes.
- The core muscles engage.
- Their back lifts.
- Their withers lift.
- Finally, the angle of the neck and head changes naturally as a result of all of these other changes.

Their back will stop hollowing, which will enable them to carry their rider more easily and help to avoid them getting back problems. They will be able to carry themselves and they will feel light and relaxed under their rider. There will be no feeling of heaviness in the hands and the horse should be able to carry out the movements we ask easily.

Collection doesn't look the same for all horses, because different breeds are built differently, but all horses can give it to us if we ask them in the right way.

If we concentrate on working through specific exercises that encourage them to step under more deeply with their hind legs, in groundwork and ridden work, and without trying to force a shape on them, they will find collection and self-carriage themselves.

The recipe for self-carriage is relaxation + balance + posture + harmony – with just a sprinkle of confidence!

You won't need to carry out any lateral work in the early tests in your dressage career. But the irony is that if you are doing a walk-trot-canter test and the judge says you need more collection, then at home you actually do need to teach your horse lateral movements!

Movements that will help improve your horse's level of collection.

- Backup exercises (there are many fun types!)
- Backwards circles
- Circles with one hind leg stepping under deeply
- Leg yields
- Shoulder out
- Shoulder in

- Sideways
- Transitions using the hindquarters
- Spirals
- Teardrops
- Halt and backup
- Trot, halt and backup
- Canter, trot, halt and backup
- Hindquarters in

The biggest takeaway I'd love you to get from his book is that collection is achieved by teaching your horse lateral movements – and not by pulling on the reins.

I have included some useful lateral work in the ridden exercises in this book that will help your horse to collect and find self-carriage. They are a good way to work on correct muscle development. They will also develop balance in yourself and your horse.

If anything starts to feel like hard work, or a bit of a struggle, stop to take stock. Be ready to go back a few steps. Go slower, and take a few minutes to figure out how you can make the lesson easier for your horse to understand.

Riding exercises for dressage training

Here are my top tips to keep in mind when you are riding:

6 ways to improve your skills today

Focus

Recently I was watching the warm up arena for the Working Equitation Championships in Golega, Portugal. There were a lot of Lusitano horses and crossbreds there, and it was magic to watch them practise the movements from flying lead changes every few strides, piaffe, passage, garrocha work, canter pirouettes and so on.

While the riders were incredibly talented, you could also see that they were working really hard. Most were staring at their horse's heads, changing their posture, moving their legs etc. Even though I was sitting in a stand at the side of a large arena, it was easy to see most of the cues they were using while they rode.

Then something amazing happened. A new rider on a large grey Lusitano came into the arena. He looked like a nice rider, with smaller cues than the other riders were using. Also he was riding one handed – which involves a higher level of riding skills than riding with two hands (try it sometimes!) His horse had a lot of energy, but also looked more calm and relaxed than most of the horses. And the rider wasn't looking down at his horse's head that much. It sounds like a small thing, but it really looked so different to the other riders in the warmup. So I decided to watch him for a while and see what would happen.

As he passed another rider on a bay Lusitano, they smiled at each other, stopped their horses and then shook hands on horseback. It seemed like they were old friends. And then the magic happened.

They decided to ride side by side in this large warm up arena, both doing the same movements. It was one of the most magical things I've ever seen in my life. I could not see any of the cues the rider on the grey used. His hands did not move. Not once did he look at his horse's head. Instead as the two riders cantered around side by side doing all sorts of exercises from canter half pass to flying lead changes, to one doing piaffe while the other did a canter pirouette around him... the rider on the grey looked at the crowd. He smiled at people he recognised sitting in the stands.

He had no tension in his body. Even though he was doing a canter pirouette, his posture looked like he was just walking his horse. No stress, no leg movements, no tension. It was the complete opposition of every other rider in the arena. He literally looked like he was doing nothing in the saddle, just riding around and admiring the views. All while his horse underneath him was doing these fabulous, relaxed movements.

He was the first rider I've ever watched perform these very high level movements with complete relaxation while looking around at the crowd watching him.

My takeaway from this moment was to look up, which has huge collection benefits.

When we look down, as our head is very heavy, we put more of our weight on our horse's front two legs. This is the opposite of collection, where we're trying to transfer some weight from the forelegs to the hind legs. So by looking down you're making it more difficult for your horse to collect.

Secondly, looking where we are going is another way to communicate to our horse where we want them to go. It's another valuable cue we can use as riders. It means we can make our other cues smaller, which makes us better riders.

How you breathe affects your horse a lot.

Just breathe

This sounds obvious but pay attention to your breathing. Are you breathing less than normal? Or faster? Thinking about breathing normally can have a massive effect on how your horse feels. Do you finish a dressage test out of breath or with a red face? You might have stopped breathing.

Tiny cues can have a big impact

Your horse can feel **tiny cues.**

Be conscious of how your body affects how your horse moves. Prepare your horse for corners and changes of direction by looking ahead and feeling the movement through your body. If you drop your inside hip very, very slightly you might be surprised to feel your horse bend around your inside leg, without you needing to ask with your reins! Never underestimate how smart your horse is. They feel every change in posture in your body when you are riding.

Use your hands less

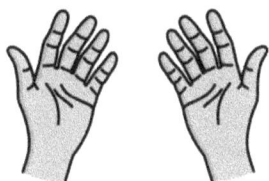

Use less pressure with your hands.

A great horse person has great hands

Be aware of using your hands too much. If you end up pulling on your reins you risk unbalancing your horse, causing them to lose soft flexion. If your horse doesn't quite understand what you want the answer is never more pressure. You might need to 'explain' by thinking about moving another part of their body. For example, if you are trying shoulder in along the side of the arena and your horse is falling in away from the rail – the answer isn't to pull them out with your hand, but to push them out with your inside leg.

Use your legs less

If you feel as if your legs are working hard, you are using them too much. A lot of people don't realise this – but if you use your legs too much you will inhibit your horse's ability to move freely.

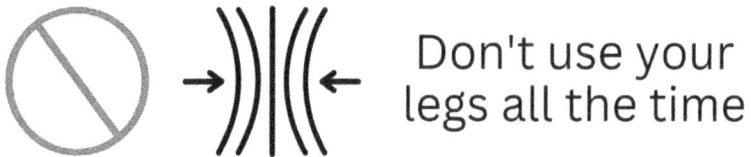

Don't use your legs all the time

Or you'll just teach your horse to ignore them

When your horse steps forward, the ribs swing out giving the hind leg room to step fully forward. As you ride you can feel the ribs swinging out as the hind hooves leave the ground. This means that if you restrict the movement through the ribs and barrel you will slow the hind legs down. If you need your horse to move faster, try swinging your legs in time with the movement of their body, with a bit more energy, and see what happens.

Be 100% on or 100% off

Always ride 'actively', whether in the arena or out on the trail/hacking. Be present for your horse and both of you will stay more alert and be less shocked if something unexpected happens. It means that you and your horse will also be developing your fitness and skills as you go.

I was riding at a clinic in Australia a few years ago with an excellent trainer who had an approach I really liked. He said you're either 100% focused, or you're completely relaxed. 100% focus involves thinking of your posture, being very aware of every movement your body makes including tiny movements of your fingers on the reins, and complete 100% concentration on your horse. You're not on your phone, talking to a friend while you ride, or thinking about what's for dinner. You are truly in the moment and working hard mentally. It is completely clear to the horse that they need to tune into your every movement. Every little movement you make means something to the horse. You'll find your horse listening to you more and responding to smaller cues.

Then you can be 100% relaxed. You can relax your entire body and have loose reins. You can slouch in the saddle. You can talk to a friend. You can plan your dinner menu. It is completely clear to the horse that they can relax and don't need to tune into your every movement.

This approach works so well for both horses and riders, but it's not easy. Most riders don't live in this 100/0 approach. They might ride at a 60% focus. They're asking their horse to do things, but their mind isn't totally there. When they relax, they don't go to zero. Maybe they go to 25%. So the horse still thinks they have to focus a bit... and the horse never gets time off. If your horse works really hard for 5 minutes, give them a minute or two to totally relax and think about things.

This 100/0 approach involves more energy and focus from us as riders, but makes life much easier for your horses, improves our riding skills and will help you reach your goals faster.

Revisit the basics regularly

Don't push you and your horse along too quickly. If something doesn't go quite right, be prepared to go back to basics to put the right building blocks in place.

For example, if your horse is nervous, lacks confidence, has poor brakes, shakes his head, doesn't like the bit... don't just keep riding 20m circles and wonder why you never get any better. Find totally new exercises and approaches to fix that exact issue. This may be new groundwork, a dentist visit or a saddle check.

If you've got a problem, fix it. Don't ignore it.

Dressage riding exercises

Breathing

Our breathing has a surprisingly powerful influence on our horses. If your horse is getting worried or tense, check in with yourself. Is your breathing shallow or rapid? Can you feel your own heart pumping? Stop, pause, concentrate on slowing your breathing down and feeling calm. Try out this simple thing next time you're riding in the arena:

Have your horse working around the outside of the arena in a nice working trot. Note their pace and the tempo of their hooves hitting the ground. Without changing anything about your hands or the rest of your body – start to count your breaths. Breathe in for a count of three. Breathe out for a count of three. Keep doing this as you trot along. I'll bet you will feel a change in your horse. You will probably note a change of tempo in the hooves hitting the ground. You might also notice other things, your horse might drop their head, or give a big breath out themselves. Hopefully you will both start to feel relaxed.

This is just an interesting observation that you should remember, it might help you when you're out and about at competitions.

Your hands (and fingers)

There's a lot of talk about how a 'contact' should feel to the rider. I've been shocked to hear it described as like a bag of sugar in each hand – that would be far too much for me!

A nicer description is that a good contact (I like to call it a connection or communication) should feel like a private conversation between ourselves and our horse.

But how do we know how that conversation sounds to the horse?

This is an exercise for you to do without your horse. You'll need a helpful friend, but they don't need to be a horse person. Get your horse's bridle. Stand in front of your friend with your back towards them and put the reins over your head and down your back so that they can hold them. Hold your hands up, with thumbs upwards. Rest the bridle over your forearms and rest the bit in the crook where your thumb joins your fingers. So that you are doing your best to re-create a horse wearing a bridle.

Ask your friend to see if they can get you to walk forward, turn right and left, stop and back up. Even if they are a horse person this might be interesting – how does it feel to you? Stop, ask your friend to change their grip on the reins so that all of their fingers, including the little finger, rest on top of the reins. Ask them to try again, but to see if they can make you understand just by moving their little finger, ask them to see how little they can do to make you turn right and left and stop. I am confident that it won't take much. Does this give pause for thought about how you use your hands when you ride your horse? If you can feel such tiny movements on quite a strong part of your hand, do you think your horse could respond to them too?

Common hand position mistake

Something to be aware of – it seems to be quite common in some styles of training for instructors to teach riders to drop their hands down, to rest on their thighs, to supposedly encourage a correct contact and outline. Even by saying this they show that they are wrongly focussing on the head rather than the powerhouse that is the horse's hind end...

A well-fitted bit should sit comfortably in the horse's mouth. It should not aggravate the bars, or the palate or any part of the mouth. When the rider picks up the reins the horse should just feel that in the sensitive corners of their lips. If a rider has a contact on the bit, and then puts their hands holding the reins down on their thighs the effect is not kind. Their hands pull the bit down onto the bars of the horse's mouth, causing at the least discomfort, but likely pain. After that any effect they have on what the horse does with their head is simply down to 'pain compliance' - never justifiable, not even to win a competition.

The warm up

Don't forget
the **warmup**.

When we start to ride our horses it is very important we give them 10-15 minutes in walk to warm up. This is even more important if it's a cold day, if your horse has been just taken out of a stable, or if your horse is a little older, and not as young as they once used to be.

Allowing your horse time to warm up their muscles at the start of each session puts them in the best place to prepare for the dressage exercises you want to teach them. Warming up your horse's muscles at the start of each session reduces the chances of injury.

Think of when you go for a walk. It could take 5-10 minutes to warm up your muscles.

The good news is that you can still do a lot of work during these 15 minutes. All of the exercises in the previous few pages – from improving your breathing, concentrating on your posture and focus, and being more subtle with the use of your hands are great things to work on during this part of your time riding your horse.

Straight lines

It may sound obvious that we need to be able to ride in straight lines. However many of us will realise, either in the arena or when watching a video back, that what we thought was straight was in fact not very straight at all! Every time you ride, think about your straight lines being truly straight. Look up and ahead straight towards where you are going. Think about your horse being straight underneath you, between your hands and legs. Try this for practise in the arena:

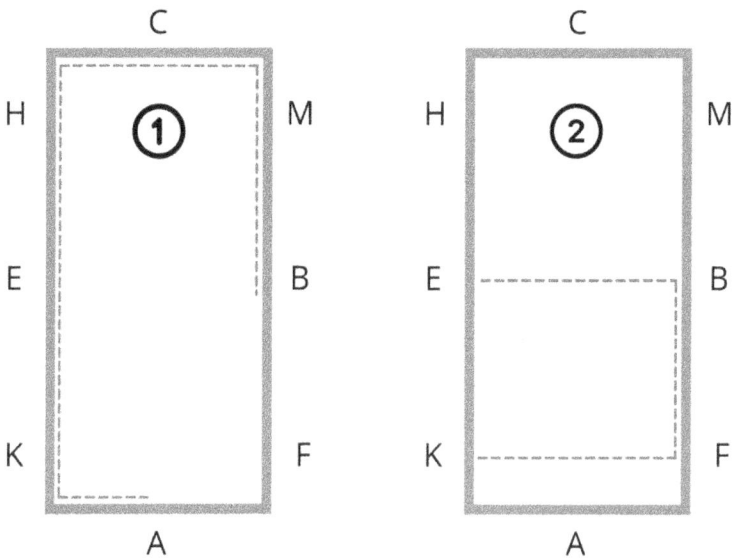

Enter the arena at A or C and first of all turn to use the rail for guidance. Look up and ahead into a corner and ride straight towards it. Make a tidy, accurate turn and ride along the long side in straightness. If you feel your horse getting crooked, don't try to correct it with more rein pressure as that will pull them off balance. Check that you are straight and looking forward yourself and use your legs to ask your horse to stay straight. Your hands are there to steady your horse and gently remind them to keep their head straight. The rest of the horse will follow.

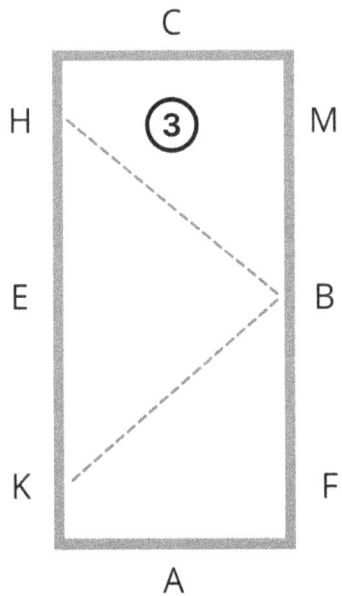

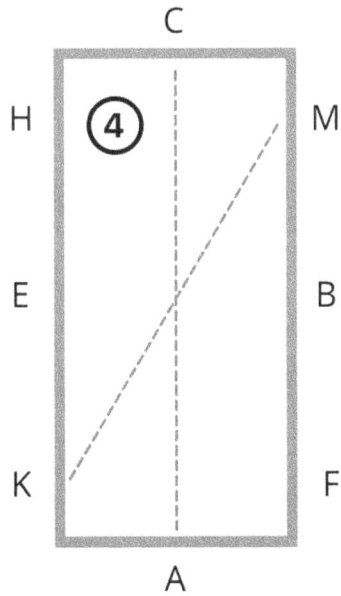

When you are happy along the rail, start to leave it and travel across the arena. Start with short straight lines, for example from K – F – B – E and K – B – H. When that is going great progress to long lines such as K – M and C – A.

Speed exercises

This is a great way to connect with your horse, and improve your cues and focus together.

①	②	③	④
10 steps normal walk	10 steps fast walk	10 steps normal walk	10 steps slow walk

*Repeat the same in **trot and canter***

Step 1: Ride 10 steps in a normal walk.

Step 2: Ride 10 steps in a very fast walk.

Step 3: Ride 10 steps in a normal walk.

Step 4: Ride 10 steps in the slowest walk possible.

This improves your communication to the horse and encourages you to use your whole body to communicate to your horse - not just the reins.

Improving your horse's energy and impulsion

The impulsion of the horse is greatly influenced by the rider's intent. The easiest way I've found to improve my horse's impulsion is to follow this simple exercise.

Step 1: Mount your horse at the mounting block, and stand still for 10-15 seconds.

Step 2: Your plan is to have no small steps today. You want every step – beginning from step 1 – to be full of energy and impulsion. Imagine there is a 70% off sale at your favourite tack store. I want you to feel the excitement in your body and look to where the imaginary tack store is.

Step 3: When you are ready, ask your horse to walk off smartly with impulsion and energy. Remember, your horse is not allowed to take any slow steps! This is a mindset change which requires more mental energy (rather than physical energy) from the rider.

No **slow** steps

Step 4: When you want to stop this exercise, or your horse needs a break from moving with energy and impulsion, ask your horse to stand still. Loosen your reins and allow you and your horse to relax. Do not go back to a slow and lazy walk. Think all or nothing. A high energy walk, or stand still and rest.

Note: In order to have impulse a horse needs energy. If your horse either has too much energy, or too little energy, think about adjusting his feed accordingly.

Weight aids

Your seat controls the bend of the horse. Your legs control the direction.

We can influence our horse's bend by very slightly putting weight on the inside seat bone (or slightly lifting the weight off the outside seat bone) to ask them to bend their body. This is a nice way to ask for a bend, with a tiny cue, and without anyone watching being able to see what you're doing!

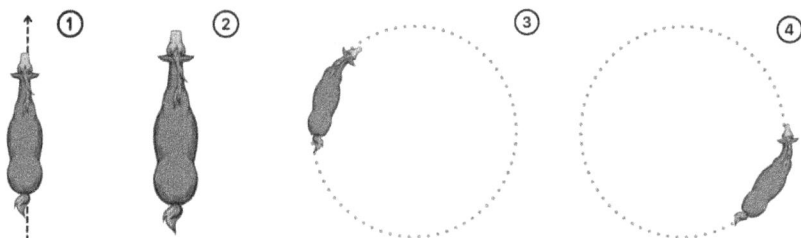

Step 1: Ride in a straight line. Be aware to carry equal weight on both seat bones.

Step 2: Halt. Ask a friend to stand a safe distance behind your horse. Make sure your weight is even on both seat bones and confirm with your friend that your shoulders are level. Now take a tiny bit of weight off your right seat bone, without moving any other part of your body. Your shoulders should not move. Confirm with your friend that they see no change in your posture. This cue is an invisible communication between you and your horse.

Step 3: Ride in a circle to the right. Your shoulders are level. As you want your horse to have a slight right bend in his body, lift up your left seat bone a fraction while keeping your shoulders level.

Step 4: Ride in a circle to the left. Your shoulders are level. As you want your horse to have a slight right bend in his body, lift up your left seat bone a fraction while keeping your shoulders level.

Step 5: Get consistent. Every time from now on you want a bend in your horse's body – doing a ride, going around a corner, shoulder out, any movement – ask for the bend with this tiny weight adjustment in your seat bones. After a while your horse will figure it out and you can change the bend in your horse's body without legs or reins. Your cues have got much smaller and your communication with your horse much more advanced. This makes everything feel easier for you and the horse.

Riding experiments

This is really worth exploring yourself to feel how the way you are carrying your weight affects the horse. Bear in mind also that if your muscles are relaxed this will affect how your weight feels to your horse. Try this:

Ride your horse around the arena in a relaxed way. Steering isn't important, they just need to keep moving forward. Look to the left – does your horse turn in that direction? Do they turn right and left? Now - let your body slump a bit and feel your weight drop down in the saddle. Does your horse stop? What happens if you straighten yourself up with energy and release your legs away from their barrel?

Always be aware of how your body affects your horse. If you are working together and your horse isn't understanding what you are asking for, check your own position and balance first. It's very easy for us to confuse them!

Bends

Here's a useful little phrase that works really well to keep your horse balanced when you're riding:

Change bend before you change direction.

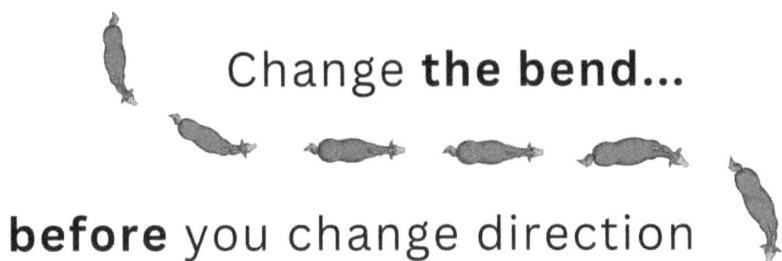

Change **the bend...**

before you change direction

When we want our horses to bend and turn for us, we should first make sure that they are able to flex their neck and turn their head in that direction. We prepare our horse to make a soft turn rather than moving straight for the reins and using them like a lever to pull the head around.

Pulling on the head will unbalance the horse. When they are turned without warning they don't have time to prepare and balance themselves. For example, if a horse is prepared it will turn as the nearest front hoof in that direction is leaving the ground. They can turn when the weight is on that hoof, but it will not be as easy for them and their movement will be unbalanced.

So, as you are planning to turn, look ahead, and then start to look where you want to go as you are a step or two away from the turn, drop your inside seat bone slightly to ask for the bend and if you need to, put a feel in the inside rein. You might find that your horse has already bent and turned!

Exercise:

Ride your horse forward at the walk. Feel for the bend with your body and reach down the rein to guide your horse to turn. Count two steps on that bend, but also be preparing to ask for bend and to turn in the opposite direction for the next two steps. So the sequence will be two steps to the left, followed by two to the right.

You will start to feel your horse getting really light, soft and responsive. When you feel that they really get it (it might not take long) introduce two steps of straight between the bends. So - two to the left, two straight, two to the right. Increase the number of steps, but if at any time your horse starts to push forward in the straight section, reduce the number of steps and make sure the bend is still there.

When you and your horse understand this expand your horizons. See how you can work in beautiful arcs and straightness all around the arena, without following markers, just by using your inside leg to ask your horse to yield out into the bend. It's a great suppling and warming up exercise, and can also be a good way to calm a horse down that is worried and help them to concentrate.

Corners

This is another thing that sounds really obvious, but when we're trying to ride our most accurate patterns in the arena things can easily start to go wrong. Horses understand the game and will have a tendency to cut corners when they are working on the rail. When you are making turns in the open area of the arena it's easy to end up with your horse turning slightly before or after where you planned. Here is something you can try to work on accurate and neat corners:

Ride out around the arena rail. Think about your horse working fully into the corner and making a good, right-angle bend. Keep in mind that accurate corners and bends come from your legs, not your hands. If you feel your horse starting to wobble or cut the corner, check your own position and push them out with your inside leg. Maintain your light, consistent contact and avoid pulling on the outside rein to try to move them out.

Useful corner tip: Instead of looking straight ahead, when you are riding clockwise experiment with looking at 11pm coming up to each corner. When you are riding anti-clockwise, experiment with looking at 1pm coming up to each corner. This extra focus on your will help your horse to stay on the outer track and not turn for the corner too soon.

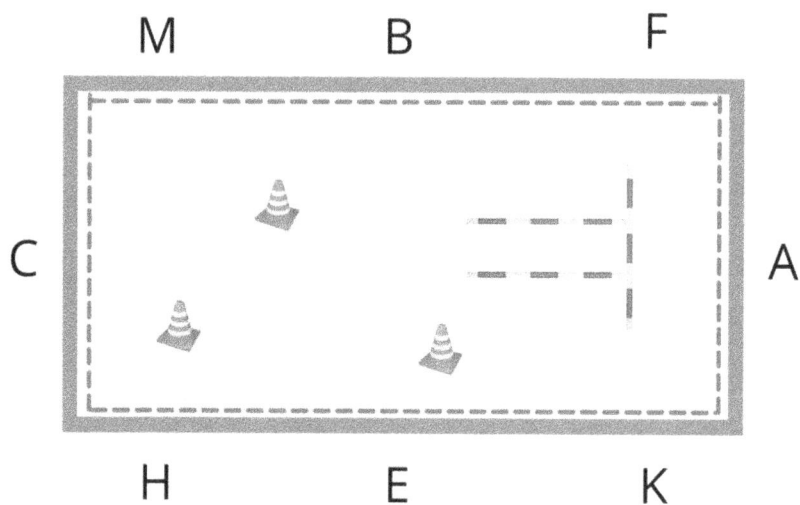

Spice things up with
cones and poles

When this is working well you can venture out into the open area. Before you start, put some markers out that you can ride around to practise. Then use exactly the same approach that you used while riding along the rail to ride accurate straight lines and bends around the markers. When that is working, ride away from the markers and ride some imaginary squares and rectangles.

Your legs - a common pitfall

One tip on your legs – If you use your legs all the time (whether it's nagging a lot to keep your horse moving forwards, or squeezing hard all the time and turning your leg muscles into jelly), you're causing yourself a big training problem. Because you use your legs all the time, your horse will start to ignore them. You've desensitised your horse to your legs. That's the last thing we want to do as dressage riders! You do not want to use your legs all the time, your horse should be able to keep travelling forward without a constant nagging from the legs. They are a cue – when you want your horse to move sideways a little, you use one leg for a moment, and then when you get that sideways step you stop using that leg and it goes back to neutral again.

If you are trying to do a nice corner using your inside leg, and your horse is ignoring it, ask yourself have you already taught your horse to ignore your leg as you use them too much already?

Accurate circles part 1

A dressage test can involve quite a few circles. When you ride your tests the judges will be looking for your circles to be the right shape (not like eggs!) and size, and for your horse to work in a balanced way, with correct bend and without falling in or looking as if they are planning to leave.

As we're riding it can be hard to tell if we are riding an exact circle. But there's a fun solution that will help both you and your horse.

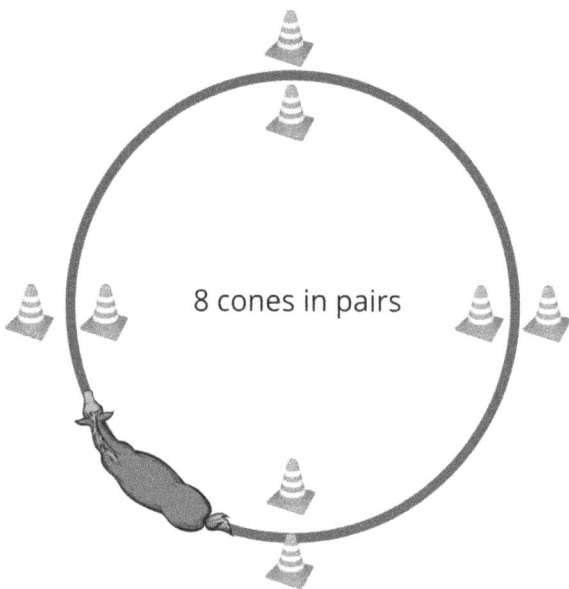

8 cones in pairs

Try riding an **8 cone circle**

Step 1: Find 8 cones.

Step 2: Put 2 cones about 2 metres apart (so you can ride through them).

Step 3: Ride through these cones in walk trot and canter without mowing any of them down. This makes it very obvious for both you and your horse where exactly you want to ride!

Accurate circles part 2

Riding circles that don't look like eggs

While paying attention to correct soft bend on circles, also be aware that you can make your circles accurate by making sure that you pass beside or through the markers and points in the arena. For example, to ride a 20 metre circle in a 40 metre arena, you could start from E, then ride through a point midway between X/L, aim for and ride past B, then mid-way between X/G and back past E.

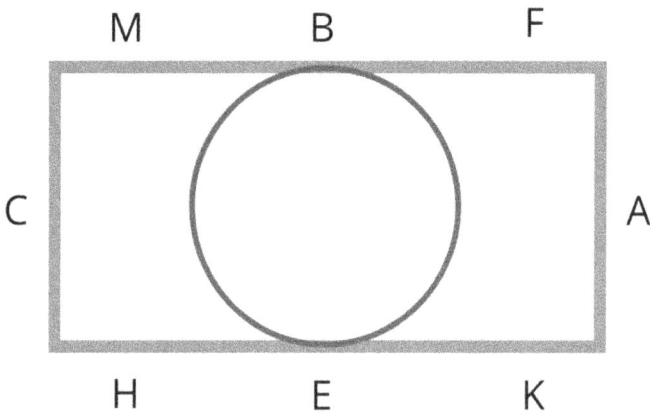

Ride a **20 metre** circle

The exercise I would suggest to help you with riding accurate circles starts with you sitting down with a drawing of your arena, with the markers included. Then draw out the riding lines for 20 metre, 15 metre and 10 metre circles.

Then take yourself and your horse out into the arena and have a try. Use your inside leg to maintain a soft bend and stop your horse falling in. Falling in is like when a motorbike goes around a corner. The whole machine leans inwards. That's what you want to avoid!

Take your outside leg back a fraction to control any outward drift of the hind end. Keep your rein contact soft and steady. Look where you are going and stay focused.

Transitions

Before doing too much work on transitions, make sure that you feel comfortable in yourself that you are confident and riding with a balanced and independent seat. If you have a tendency to tip forward, or become unbalanced in any way, it's worth working on that before doing too much on transitions.

Your horse too needs to be prepared for transitions. They will find it much easier if they are used to working with their weight on their hind end, so that they have the power and impulsion to move up a gait. Then take the two of you out into the arena and have a go:

At first your horse will be likely to find it easier to transition up a gait if you ask as you are coming out of a corner. Raise your energy, and if you need to, put your leg on to ask for more forward. Be careful that you don't inadvertently pull on the reins as your horse breaks into the trot. Just trot for a few steps, then relax, slow your body and move back to walk. Make sure that your horse doesn't come to a complete halt when you want to just walk. Gradually build on this to trot for longer distances. At first come back down to walk as you approach the next corner, but when you and your horse are finding this easy feel free to go right around the arena. The principle is the same for transitions to canter.

If your horse starts to get strong, maybe anticipating the change in gait, or being reluctant to slow down, take things back a stage. Re-establish the walk. Possibly practise some halts and backups. Practise transitioning up for just two or three steps then slowing down. Do what works for you and your horse to get together and think again.

Working on transitions is a big topic, there are so many variations! So when you have established walk, trot and canter around the rail use your creativity to take it to the next level. Can you walk across the long diagonal, transitioning to trot at X, then back to walk at the rail? How are halt to trot transitions? Or walk to canter? How about setting up a 20 metre circle in the centre of the arena with cones at 12, 3, 6 and 9 o'clock and practising accurate transitions as you pass those markers?

Transitions are great for developing impulsion in horses that are reluctant to go freely forward, and yet they will also help a horse with the opposite problem – who rushes too much. They teach horse and rider to focus and help horses to learn not to anticipate our requests.

Remember, in a dressage test, the first step in a new gait should happen when the rider's body passes the letter.

Transitions homework for a dressage test

If you're riding a dressage test and it says 'Trot at C' then you need your horse to trot at C. So here is a handy homework experiment you can do to maximise the chance of this happening!

Research with **how many steps** it takes today for a **walk to trot transition**

Step 1: Walk your horse.

Step 2: Ask your horse to trot.

Step 3: Notice what distance it takes for your horse to take the first stride of trot. Was it immediate? Was it 2 walk strides later? Was it 5 walk strides later?

If in your training, you know that currently it takes your horse 4 walk strides to transition to trot after you ask, then during your test, ask your horse to trot 4 walk strides before C, to maximise your chances of a walk-trot transition exactly at C.

Figure of 8

Let's play around with a useful exercise that gives you the opportunity to work on accurate circles, bends and transitions. Excellent for helping your horse to be supple and good for helping you and your horse to stay focussed. The most simple figure of 8 is based on two 20 metre circles:

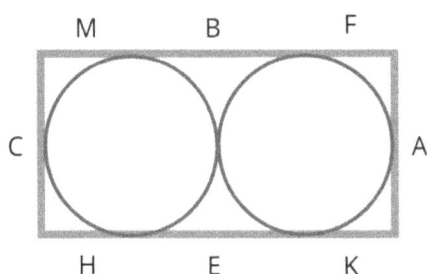

Ride a
figure of 8

Enter the arena at A. Ride a 20 metre circle. As you pass X the second time change direction and ride a 20 metre circle in the opposite direction. (If you are in a 60 metre arena you will need to adapt this slightly). Try this at a walk, trot and canter. Riding figure of 8's like this can be preparation for flying lead changes!

You can ride smaller figure of 8's. If you are considering making the circles smaller than 10 metres make sure to take your horse's physical ability into account.

Figure of 8 challenge – ride a figure of 8 with no hands! I reckon if you've worked through all of the earlier exercises you can probably do this. Give it a try and maybe surprise yourself. A 10 metre figure of 8 might be the easiest place to start, as it gives your horse less room to wander off. Put your reins on your horse's neck, or if you aren't confident to do that hold them at the buckle. Use what you have learned about focus, looking where you want to go and using your body to ride that figure of 8!

3 loop serpentines

Serpentines are a brilliant way to practise focus, accuracy and correct bend. Visualise where you will need to ride to, in the arena before you start, maybe even rehearse on foot. In a 40 metre arena for example you will aim for C – H – B – K – A. In a 60 metre arena the sequence would be the same, but you aim for the mid-point between M/R and P/F. Make sure you plan out the opposite direction as well.

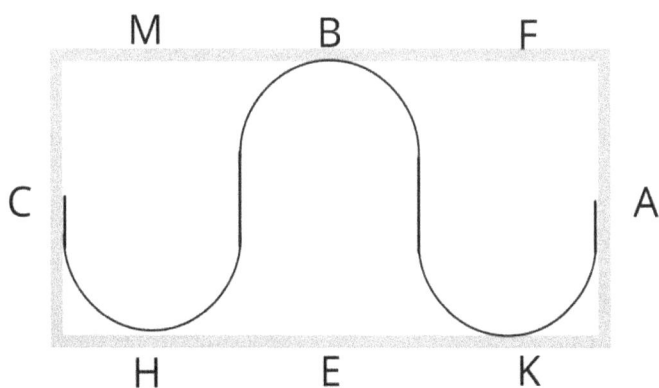

Serpentines

When I ride this exercise, my aim is to steer my horse from my body, maintaining a soft and consistent rein contact but not pulling on the reins for direction. As mentioned before, if you keep your head up and look in the direction of where you want to be it will really help. Use your inside leg to keep or enlarge the bend and your outside leg slightly back to stop the hindquarters drifting out. Here's an exercise that will help you to get started:

In serpentines you will ride your horse in an arc as you approach the side of the arena and turn away to cross through the middle. As you pass through the middle there will be a few steps of straightness. To help with accuracy when you are new to this, get hold of two jump poles, or a few cones. Use these to mark out a channel for your horse to pass through as you cross the middle of the arena (in line with A, C and X).

Teaching your horse to fall in love with corners

One common issue you hear a lot during a dressage lesson is the instructor asking the rider to actually ride into the corner, and not to cut the corners. This is a fun exercise to help your horse fall in love with going into every corner of the arena!

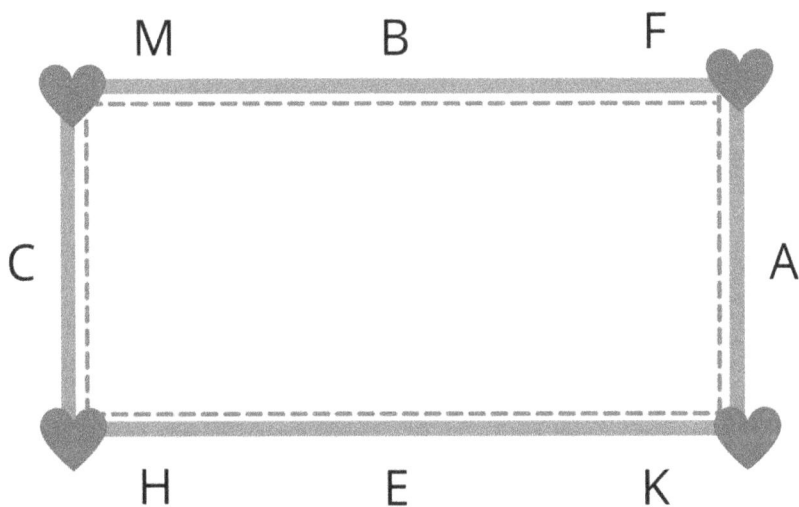

Halt at ♥ to ride deep **into the corners**

Step 1: Walk or trot in a straight line along each side.

Step 2: In each corner, stop for 30 seconds, loosen the reins and praise your horse.

Within a lap or two of the arena, you should notice improved straightness on the side of the arena, and a greater willingness to ride deep into the corners.

Trot diagonals

The trot is a two-beat gait, so when we do a rising trot we rise, we sit, we rise we sit and so on. In order to do this equally (instead of for example, always rising when your horse's near fore is rising, instead of 50% when near fore is rising, and 50% when off fore is rising), we want to do our rising trot on the correct diagonal.

This is just a fancy way to say we want to be rising out of the saddle when our horse's outside front leg is leaving the ground. And we want to be sitting back into the saddle when our horse's outside front leg is coming back to the ground.

But here's the problem. When you're riding, how do you know when that outside front leg is moving up or down? You can lean over and peer down, which does horrible things to your posture and you'll lose marks in a dressage test.

You could look down and watch your horse's outside shoulder, which will put more weight on your horse's withers and make it more difficult for your horse to collect himself.

Thankfully there is a simple way I use, that allows you to get your trot diagonals perfect every time, and has no negative impact on your posture. No one will know what you're doing and they should be highly impressed when you keep getting your diagonals right every time! So here it is.

Use your legs to **feel the swing** of your horse's body

Step 1: Walk your horse on a large circle or rectangle, and relax your body. Feel your legs naturally swing a little from side to side.

Step 2: As you ride, notice each time your inside leg swings in.

Step 3: Each time your inside leg swings in, say (or think) the word UP. Do this for a few minutes.

Step 4: When you're confident with this, try sitting trot with your horse. As you ride, notice each time your inside leg swings in.

Step 5: Each time your inside leg swings in, say (or think) the word UP. You are still doing sitting trot.

Step 6: As you are trotting around, now rise out of the riding each time you say UP. You are now doing rising trot (UK), or posting the trot (USA), on the correct diagonal.

Changing diagonals: As you trot, sit for 2 beats instead of 1 beat to change the diagonal.

Trot transitions and diagonals

This is a fun exercise to combine accurate trot transitions with the correct trot diagonal.

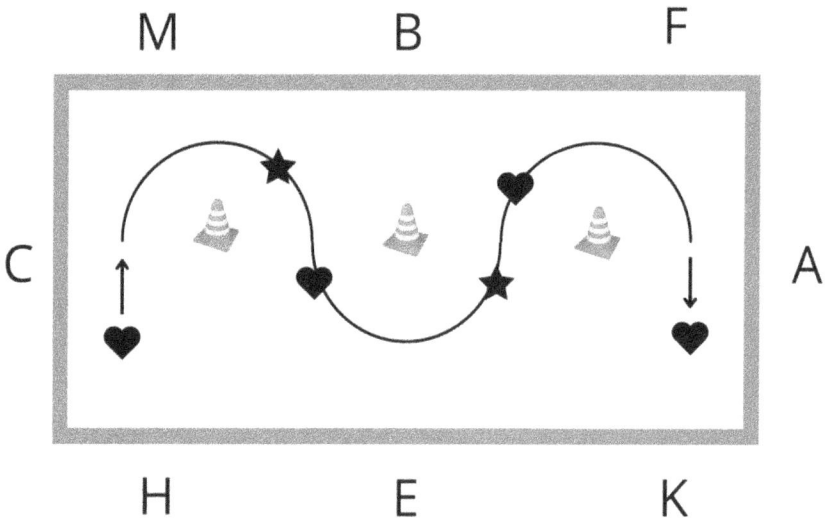

3 walk to trot transitions. Trot at the ♥. Walk at the ★

Set up 3 cones a good distance apart. Start the exercise with the correct trot diagonal. Where there is a star, go back to walk. Where there is a heart, trot on again with the correct diagonal.

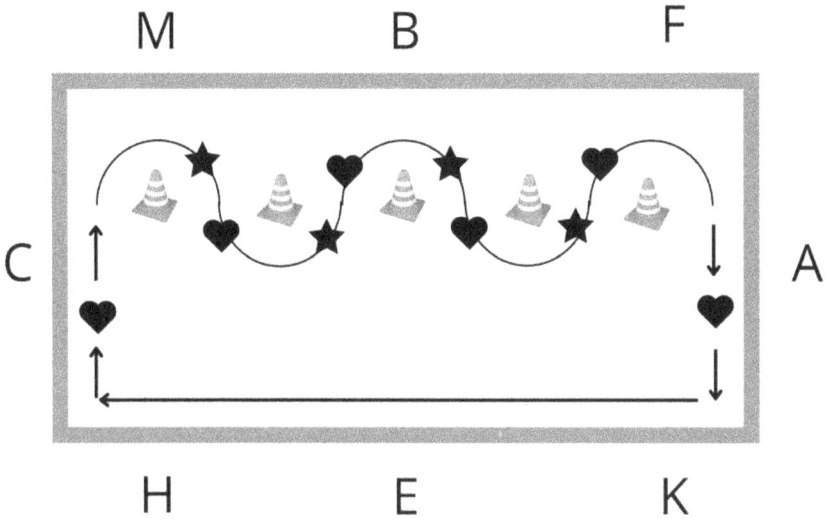

5 walk to trot transitions. Trot at the ♥. Walk at the ★

Set up 5 cones a good distance apart. Start the exercise with the correct trot diagonal. Where there is a star, go back to walk. Where there is a heart, trot on again with the correct diagonal.

You can repeat this in both directions.

Simple canter transitions

This is a nice exercise to practise your simple canter lead changes. Put out 3 cones a good distance apart. The further apart the cones are, the easier this exercise will be.

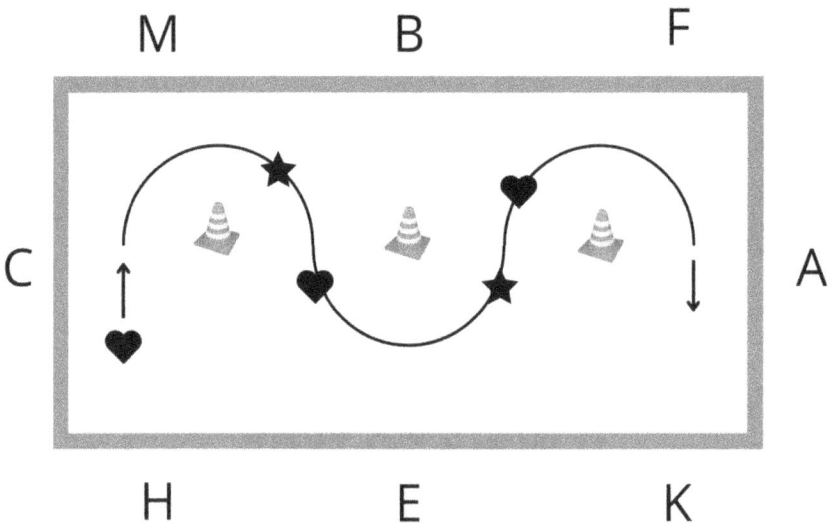

3 Simple canter transitions. Canter at the ♥. Trot at the ★

Set up 3 cones a good distance apart. Start the exercise with a canter going to the right. Where there is a star, go back to sitting trot, and then ask your horse to change the bend in his body. Where there is a heart, canter on again with the correct lead.

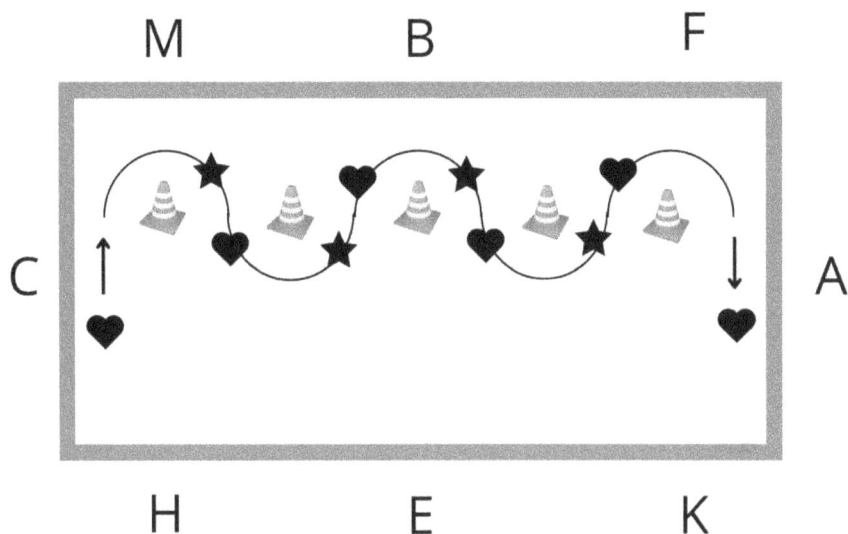

5 Simple canter transitions. Canter at the ♥. Trot at the ★

Set up 5 cones a good distance apart. Start the exercise with a canter going to the right. Where there is a star, go back to sitting trot, and then ask your horse to change the bend in his body. Where there is a heart, canter on again with the correct lead.

You can repeat this in both directions.

Ride at rest

When you and your horse have been working away together, maybe learning some new moves, testing yourselves mentally and physically – there is an important thing to do before you stop and put your horse away. Relax together and ride at rest.

Experimenting with **tiny aids**

Hold your horse's reins on the buckle, or even lay them down in their neck. Keep your energy just high enough to ask them to walk forward, but don't ask for anything more. Let them wander about where they want to go for a few minutes. Then start thinking about subtly suggesting a direction by looking in the direction you'd like to go. You can ask for bend by very slightly dropping your inside hip (just think of that seat bone being slightly heavier) and you can use your legs lightly, but you are not allowed to use your rein. Nearly everyone who tries this is surprised at how responsive their horse is. Just keep relaxed and play around like this for maybe five minutes or so, then get off your horse, loosen their girth and put them away.

Riding exercises for collection

Halt and backup

You remember how we talked about halt and backup in the groundwork exercises? When you are riding, they are also very important. Getting the halt and backup good will help your horse to become soft in your hand, transfer their weight to the hind end and balance themselves.

Walk, halt, then backup

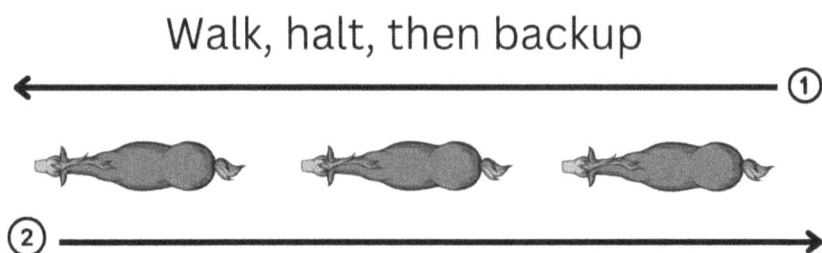

As you ride along, decide on where you want to stop and start preparing your horse a few steps before. Lower your energy, breathe out and 'stop riding'. Gently pick up on the rein if they don't stop. Think about your halt being square and your horse feeling soft in your hand. Notice how many steps it took to go from walk to halt. A good exercise would be to repeat this a few times and notice if you can reduce this number. Your horse should be able to stop from cues from your body and a vocal cue if you want to use one – without you needing to touch the reins!

When you ask for a backup first make sure that your horse feels soft in your hand and isn't pushing forward. Put enough feel in your reins to ask the horse not to walk forward, feel back with your body, add a little pressure from your legs if need be. Stop asking when your horse feels soft, if you stop when they are pushing or moving their legs all over the place, they will think that's what you want them to do.

Let's return to that halt. What do you do if your horse isn't square or they are pushing on your hands? Practise a step or maybe a few of backup. Ask for the backup, make sure it's without tension and bracing, and that you only stop when it is, and your horse is straight. If they are tense, see if you can ask your horse to turn just their head slightly left and right to release the tension in their neck, before you ask them to back up.

Pause to let them think for a minute or two. Then ask for a steady walk forward, then another halt.

Sometimes if a horse is repeatedly pushing forward when halting it's worth asking them to change the way they think about it. You could ask for backup every time they halt, just for a while, making sure that you only stop when they are soft. Do this in the arena, when you're out hacking/trail riding and even when you're handling them on the ground! When they understand, then that shouldn't be necessary any more.

10 steps exercise

Here's a great exercise on backup and halt, it works on precision and focus and is great for showing a horse how to shift their balance backward:

Ride your horse forward 10 steps at an active walk. Halt. Ask for softness in your hands (you might already have it). Ask your horse to walk back 10 steps. Repeat for 9 steps, 8 steps and so on until it's just one step. You will get to the point where your horse is so on this that you will be able to start to ask for backup, then think about forward instead and feel them softly rock underneath you – without even lifting a hoof!

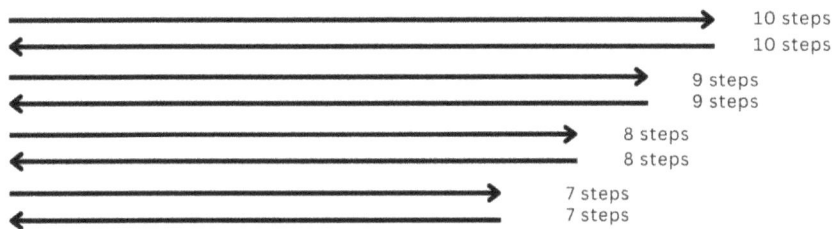

and so on, until you get to 0 steps

When you ride this exercise don't lose your precision. You are still working on softness and straightness... and don't be surprised if you feel some real collection and self-carriage!

Spirals

To ride a spiral you will establish a circle at the walk, leg yield your horse out gradually to make the circle wider, then yield them back in again to return to the original circle.

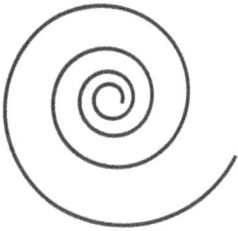

Spiral by **leg yielding**

You will use your inside leg to maintain the bend and impulsion. Use your outside leg slightly back to stop the hindquarters swinging out. A regular soft rein contact just helps to control the shoulder and stop your horse rushing, but you should not need to be forceful.

Spice up your spirals:

Ride your horse in a spiral from a 10 metre circle to a 20 metre circle at the walk. Change the bend through the middle of the circle and ride a 20 metre circle in the opposite direction. Then yield back into a 10 metre circle. Repeat. Move it up to trot. What can you do in canter?

Teardrop and shoulder control

The teardrop is a great exercise to help you to supple up your horse and practise shoulder control.

You can start this at the walk, and progress to trot when you're ready. Ride in walk along the long side of the arena. Then ride a 5 metre teardrop shape (by riding a half circle), returning to the track again, now riding in the opposite direction.

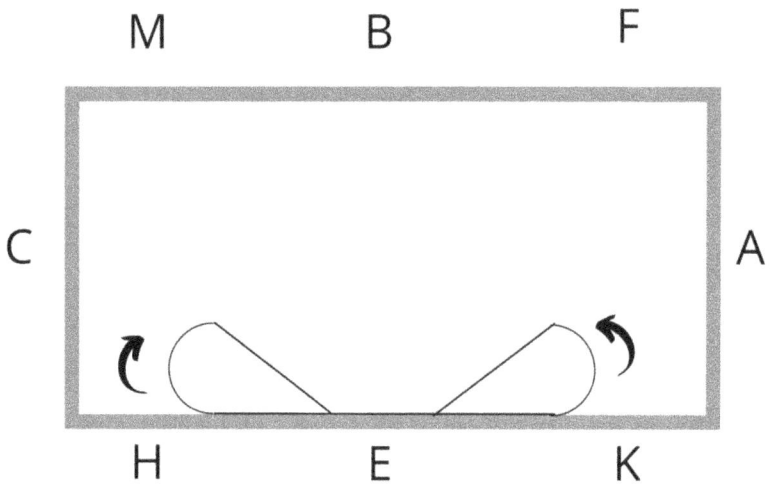

Ride a **5 metre teardrop**

There is a lot you can do with the teardrop shape. You can ride one teardrop, then carry on to the opposite long side and use another teardrop to change direction. You can ride the shape as a simple bend and ride forward, or you can leg yield into the half circle, then back to the track. Be creative and mix it up to keep life interesting.

Some advanced ideas: You can leg yield back to the arena wall. Another idea – just before you start the half circle, ride 1-2 steps of shoulder in.

Shoulder out

We have looked at how you can start this on the ground with your horse. Now it's time to repeat the same exercise in the saddle.

First we need your horse to have a little energy and to feel relaxed and confident. If your horse has zero energy this is going to be tricky because they will not have enough 'forward'. If your horse is worried or anxious, this is going to be tricky too. You are better off fixing those issues first, before you try shoulder out.

Next up you will ask your horse to walk along a fence line. You will be very aware that you are looking straight ahead, and not down at your horse's head. This is very important.

Now walk along the fence line again. This time, you will keep looking straight ahead and now you will ask your horse to create a little bend in their body towards the fence, by lifting your weight a fraction from the seat bone that is closest to the inside of the arena.

Make sure your leg which is closest to the inside of the arena is hardly touching your horse at all.

Finally, move your leg which is closest to the fence line backwards just a fraction to encourage your horse to move his hindquarters a little more towards the middle of the arena.

Use your outside leg to stop your horse drifting away from the fence.

Once you get even one step of a sideways movement stop asking your horse to go sideways and walk forwards normally, along the fence line.

Only ask for one step! Don't get greedy.

This is an athletic movement you are asking your horse to do, so just ask for a little when you begin.

Leg yield

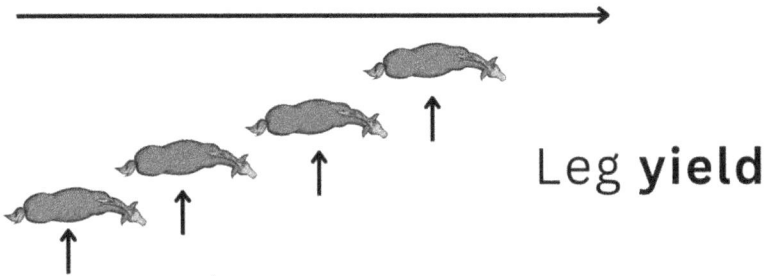

Leg **yield**

When you ask your horse to leg yield you ask them to flex slightly away from the direction of travel, and move sideways and forward at the same time. Your inside hand asks for the bend, your inside leg asks your horse to move over laterally. Your outside leg controls how far they drift over. A good leg yield should show a consistent level of lateral movement as your horse travels forward.

If you watch a horse doing a good leg yield you will see that their shoulder is travelling slightly ahead of their hindquarters, and their inside legs are crossing in front of their outside legs.

It's important to balance the sideways movement with forward. You need to keep the impulsion for this to work, if your horse slows down they are likely to grind to a halt.

Leg yield to HQ in

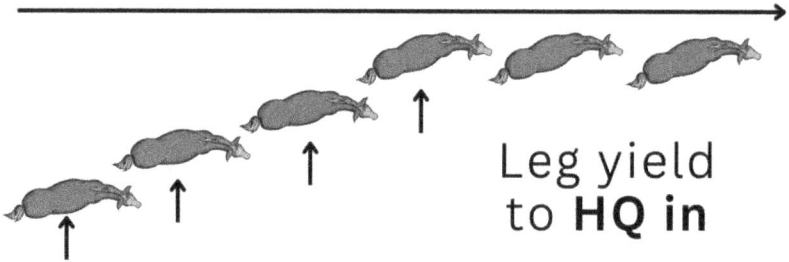

Leg yield
to **HQ in**

Ride a circle with your horse in walk. Your horse's body will have a slight bend through it, the same as the circle he is travelling on. When you are coming towards the fence line, ask your horse to leg yield to the fence. To do this you'll look where you are going, open your outside leg so the horse can move that way, and just touch gently with your inside leg.

Note: Your inside leg is the leg on the side of the bend. So furthest from the fence. Your outside leg is the leg on the outside of the bend so nearest to the fence.

Remember to lift your outside seat bone a fraction.

As your horse comes beside the fence, keep everything exactly the same, the same bend in the horses body, and do two things:

- Reduce the cue with your inside leg.

- Put your outside leg back to ask your horse to feel his hindquarters inside the arena.

Your aim is to ride a step or two along the fence line, with your horse's two front feet on the outer track, and his two hind feet slightly more inside, with a bend in his body. This is called hindquarters in. It's a tricky exercise for the horse physically, but just play with it, have fun and only ask for a step then walk forwards in a straight line along the fence to finish.

When you've got this you can repeat this in sitting trot. Don't look for perfection. Don't use force or overuse your legs. Just ask your horse gently, and accept what they offer. We want the horse to understand the cues, we do not want to just physically force the horse's body into position. Working with the horse's mind to teach him will result in much better dressage test performances.

Trot to halt

This is a fun exercise that will both improve your brakes and your horse's collection. I like to use the voice command 'Ho'. *It's up to you to use this if you want to.*

When I say 'Ho', I say it like someone has just punched me in the stomach and all the air is leaving my chest.
'HhhooooooooooooooooooooOOO'

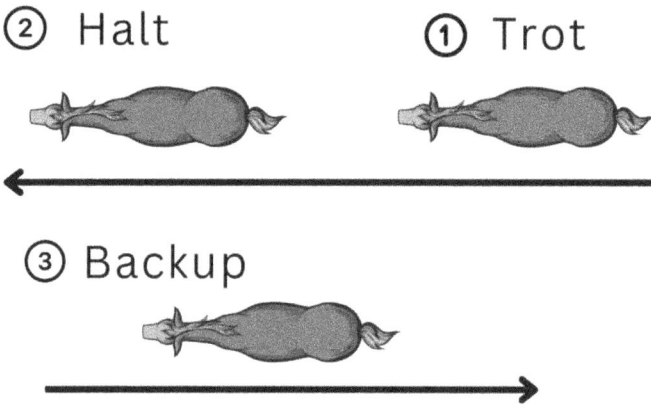

② Halt   ① Trot

③ Backup

Trot, halt, backup

Step 1: Halt and backup. The steps to do this are detailed a few pages back.

Step 2: Walk, halt, and backup. When you want to ask your horse to halt, say 'Ho' breathe out deeply, sit on the back pockets of your jeans and relax your entire body. All of these cues should be enough for your horse to stop. Count how many steps it takes from asking to stopping. If you go over 5 steps, you can gently close your fingers over the reins to ask for a halt. Then backup.

Repeat this exercise (walk, halt, backup) for a minute until you can reduce the number of steps it takes to go from walk to halt.

The reason we do it this way, with very little rein, is that we want our horses to stop using their hindquarters instead of their forequarters. To stop using their hindquarters, they need to transfer more weight to the hindquarters. This is the start of collection.

Step 3: When step 2 is good (which may take a week or more, be patient!) move onto step 3. Trot, halt, backup. The cues are the same. When you want to ask your horse to halt, say 'Ho' breathe out deeply, sit on the back pockets of your jeans and relax your entire body. All of these cues should be enough for your horse to stop. Count how many steps it takes from asking to stopping. If you go over 7 steps, you can gently close your fingers over the reins to ask for a halt. Then backup. Repeat this exercise (trot, walk, halt, backup) for a minute until you can reduce the number of steps it takes to go from trot to halt.

Again, we are teaching the horse's mind, so that they understand the cues and do the physical movements themselves. We don't need to pull on the reins to physically stop them (usually with weight on the forehand). Instead they understand what we are asking, and stop their bodies by themselves, using their hindquarters.

Backup circles

The backing up exercise is a great way to improve your horse's posture and collection, as when you ask your horse to walk backwards they have to shift weight onto the hindquarters (which is how collection starts).

So here is another interesting backup exercise.

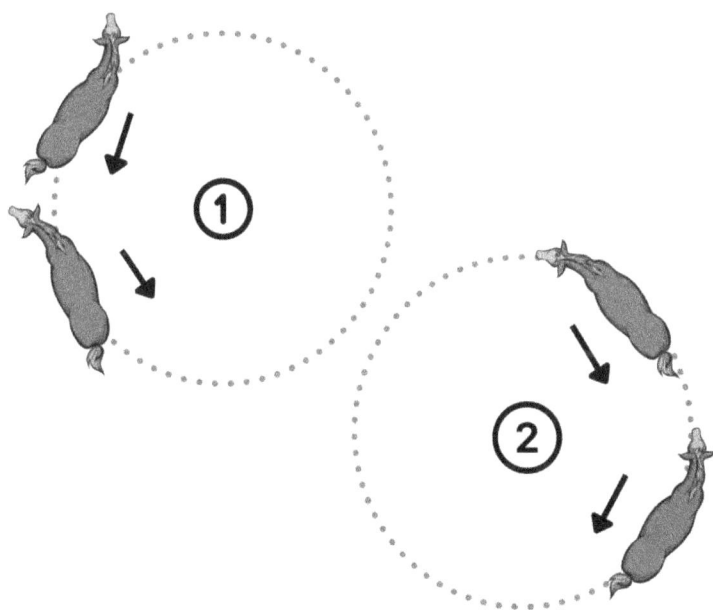

Backup circles

Moderate difficulty:

Ask your horse to back up in a circle. Start with a few steps backwards, and then turn it into a backwards circle. As you back up in the circle, your horse can look out of the circle, and then the bend in his body will be the opposite to the circle he is doing (this is the easiest way to start this for your horse). Start with half a circle, and work up to a full circle. Give your horse lots of rests and praise.

Then try it going backwards in the other direction.

After you have ridden a circle backwards in both directions, look at the size of the circles. Larger backwards circles are easier for your horse. The smaller they can make the circles, the better your horse is improving his bend and collection. Accept whatever the horse offers you, as you can't force this. But you'll see your circle size improve over time.

Also notice the difference in size between your backwards circles in both directions. Usually they are different sizes. Larger circle = your horse found that way more difficult physically. So be patient. Sometimes bodywork like a physio or a Masterson practitioner can be helpful here too.

Advanced difficulty:

Note: For this exercise you need to be able to control your horse's hindquarters, and be working on hindquarters in a little.

Ask your horse to back up in a circle. Start with a few steps backwards, and then turn it into a backwards circle. As you back up in the circle, your horse looks into the circle, and the bend in his body will be the same as the circle he is doing. Start with half a circle, and work up to a full circle. Give your horse lots of rest and praise.

Then try it going backwards in the other direction.

After you have ridden a circle backwards in both directions, look at the size of the circles. Larger backwards circles are easier for your horse. The smaller they can make the circles, the better your horse is improving his bend and collection. Accept whatever the horse offers you, as you can't force this. But you'll see your circle size improve over time.

Also notice the difference in size between your backwards circles in both directions. Usually they are different sizes. Larger circle = your horse found that way more difficult physically. So be patient.

180 degree turn then backup

This is another fun exercise to engage the hindquarters and use backup to improve collection.

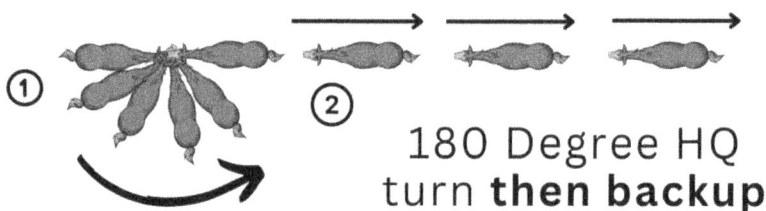

180 Degree HQ turn **then backup**

Step 1: Ride in walk along the fence line.

Step 2: Halt, using the subtle cues we've been working on in previous exercises.

Step 3: Ask your horse to move their hind legs 180 degrees, while their front legs stay still, until they are parallel to the fence line, facing the other direction.

Step 4: As you are finishing the last step or two of the hindquarters, start to think about backup. Then backup a few steps, staying parallel to the fence.

The secret to this exercise is having your horse thinking backwards while moving his hind legs. When your horse thinks backwards, the weight shifts to those hind legs. The movement of the hind legs starts to feel smooth, like a train going around a corner on a railway line. To help the horse do this, you've got to also be thinking backwards as you do this exercise. When we think of a movement, our bodies actually change slightly and our horses can feel this and understand this.

The goal is for this movement to feel as smooth as butter, and for the horse to flow backwards by himself during the final backup. By the end, you should just be able to do this using a tiny leg cue to move the hind legs, and a backwards thought to ask your horse to take a few steps backwards. Our goal is always tiny invisible cues.

Sideways over two poles

Place 2 poles on the ground, parallel to each other and 4 to 5 meters apart.

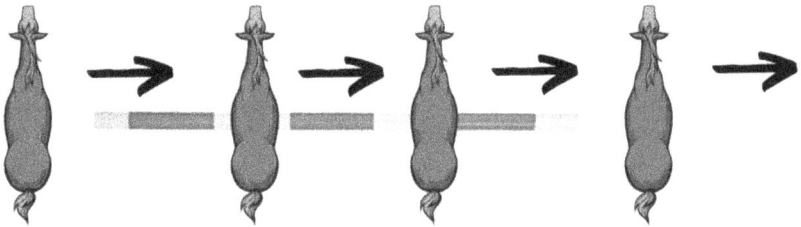

1 Sideways over 2 poles

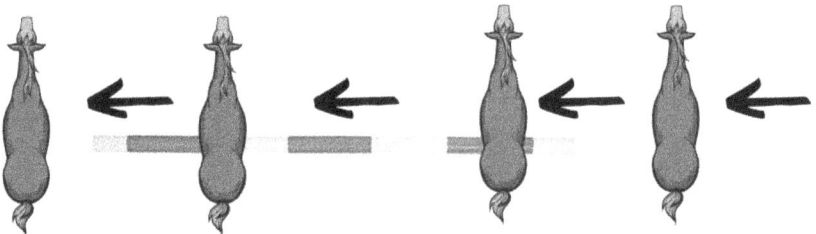

Exercise 1: Ask your horse to walk sideways to the left over the first pole, then walk forward then walk sideways to the right over the

second pole. Asking your horse to move sideways causes a weight shift from the forelegs to the hind legs.

Tip: Think about the pole on the ground staying just behind your foot while you are sitting in the saddle.

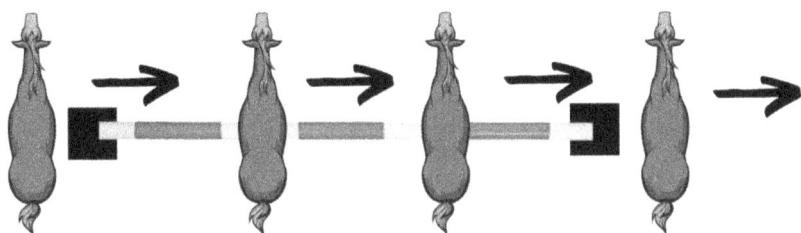

Sideways over 2 raised poles

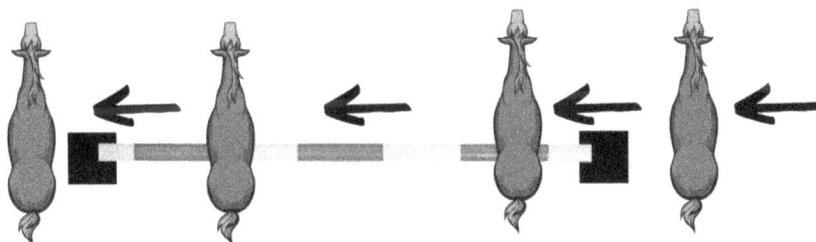

Exercise 2: Repeat this exercise, but this time raise the poles up a few inches off the ground.

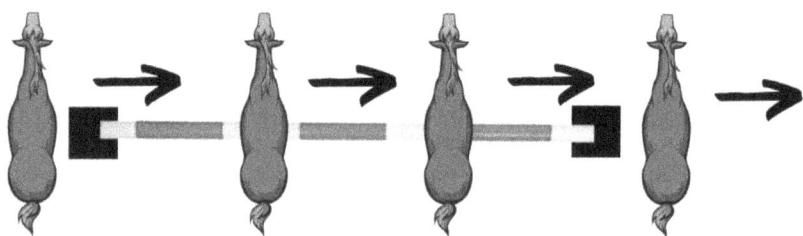

③ Sideways over 2 raised poles holding both reins in one hand

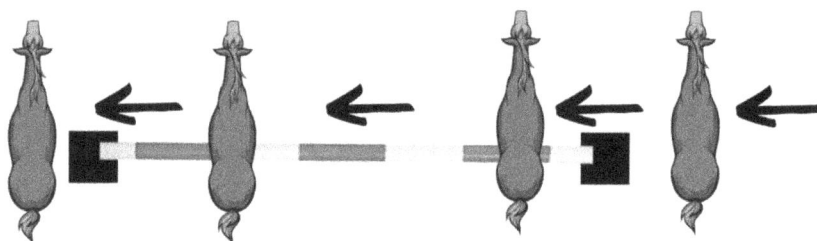

Exercise 3: Repeat this exercise, but this time raise the poles up a few inches off the ground and ride this exercise with both of your reins in one hand.

Be creative

Don't get too serious! Add obstacles to your dressage training - cones, barrels, poles. Perform your dressage movements to, around and over these obstacles to give the horse a different focus, other than a blank, boring arena. These are a fun way to spice up your training sessions.

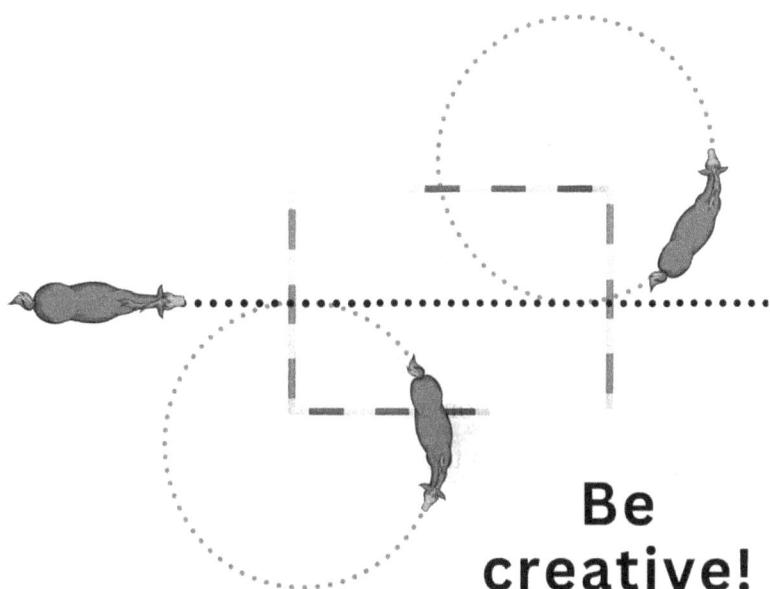

Be creative!

Remember dressage is supposed to be fun!

Getting out and competing

The big day is approaching - you've been training, you've been planning, you've been practising and the time to get out and show what you and your horse can do is nearly here! Here are a few things to think about before you go. The better your planning and preparation the easier you will find it on the day and the more relaxed you will feel.

Volunteer at a local dressage event.

Volunteer to be a scribe at a few local shows. This is where you sit with the judge and write down their comments into the test score sheets. You can learn a lot & begin to understand what the judges are looking for, and common mistakes other dressage riders are making that you can avoid in the future.

Mindset for the dressage rider

How do you feel when you think about what's ahead of you in the dressage test arena? Do you feel fired up and ready to go or do you feel nervous and are possibly regretting filling out your entry form?

Are you out there to win or are you just hoping to enjoy yourself? I would suggest that you put all thoughts of winning out of your mind and instead visualise you and your horse being relaxed together, having fun and just doing the best that you can do. If you concentrate on not putting yourself under too much pressure you might be surprised at what you achieve!

Here are some tips for having a positive and successful attitude while you train for your dressage competitions and to keep in mind while you're at the shows:

Complete one or more level below what you are training with your horse at home. This will take the pressure off you and your horse, reduce your stress level & and help you have a more fun and enjoyable day out.

Sometimes we get frustrated with our horses. Sometimes it feels as if they are doing things deliberately to irritate us. But don't label your horse. I think that the names we call our horses, sometimes even as a joke, influence how we feel about them. If your horse is having a bad day - they're just a horse being a horse. Horses don't set out to upset us and spoil our day, they just don't work like that. So rather than labelling our horses as being naughty, being a pillock, a bozo, a woose, or the village idiot - let's turn that upside down and call them clever boy, top mare, special horse, my hero and similar.

Don't take it too hard if things don't go to plan. Let's say you're riding your test in an outdoor arena and it starts lashing down with rain. Your horse tucks its tail between its hindquarters, turns their back to the rain and refuses to move. Just smile and relax, give them a rub. It's just one of those things. Chalk it up to experience. Getting frustrated never helps.

Don't be too hard on yourself. Let's imagine that you are halfway through your test and it's going great. Then the rider in the next arena gets bucked off and her horse jumps over the markers and ends up in your arena making friendly overtures to your mount. Your judge stops your test while the horse is caught and you're asked to restart when the excitement is over. You're flustered, you've lost focus, and your horse is calling for their new friend. You re-start the test but it doesn't go well. You might feel disappointed in yourself and that you've let your horse down. On the other hand, you could celebrate the fact that you and your horse survived the excitement, stayed together, and got the job done.

Judges' comments can be interesting. Sometimes they can be really helpful and give you some constructive criticism that will help you to do better next time. On the other hand, they can be negative and confusing. You might have an aspect of your riding that you were particularly pleased with, then see an opposite view on the score sheet. Let's say for example you were thrilled that your horse was so relaxed for their 20 metre circles, but the judge comments that there was a lack of impulsion. It's not worth crying over, tomorrow is another day (and remember it's meant to be fun!). At the end of one test I saw recently, the judge said a few words to the rider and the rider rode out of the arena crying. It was horrible to see. But it can happen.

Remember, the only true judge of you as a rider is your horse.

Whether it's training at home or riding in a competition keep your horse's age and experience in mind. This is very important. For a start, horses' bodies mature slowly and they aren't really grown up until at least six or seven years old. Mentally some mature more quickly than others, but physically that is not the case. Don't do too much too soon. You won't do any harm by proceeding slowly, but you can set you and your horse back quite a way by pushing on too fast. You will see people demanding a lot of young horses, even when they are only three or four years old. Don't be tempted to copy them, whatever the breed, and whatever training their horses had, they all mature at the same rate.

Make sure that you go to small, quite informal venues for your first competitions, to avoid over facing your horse and yourself. Try not to put your horse into situations where they will feel stressed and lose their confidence, progress gradually to larger competitions and venues.

Be patient when you're teaching your horse something new. Give them short breaks during the process to think about it. Praise them verbally when they get it right - they will understand! Remember that our goal is not just to work with our horses physically but also to educate their minds. We need to strive to be the best teacher that we can for them. Once a horse mentally understands what is being asked of them they will find it much easier to perform movements with lightness and softness. This will make your job much easier as a rider as you will have a mental connection, be able to use light physical cues, and be working with your horse.

KISS – Keep It Simple Stupid. Break the more complex tasks down into smaller, calmer, simpler tasks. For example – even something as simple as a 20 metre circle is an exercise in precision that can be broken down. First, you need to be able to ride accurately to the arena markers to make sure that the size of the circle is accurate. Then you need to be able to ask your horse for soft flexion and have them maintain it without forcefully holding them in shape. You also need to be prepared for them to drop their shoulder in the bend, and be able to remedy that. Put it all together and you have the perfect 20 metre circle!

Remember to practise everything in both directions and on both sides. Let's say you've been working on a leg yield on a circle to the right and it's going great. Make sure to try leg yield to the left as well. You might find it doesn't work, this is totally normal, you need to teach all of the exercises, step by step, right from the beginning on both sides.

Competitions

Competition preparation – your transport

How are you going to get there? Are you transporting yourself and your horse? Or maybe a friend is going to take you. A lot of us will be using a professional transporter. Make sure that, even if it costs money, you are using a person and transport that you feel you can trust. If you have your own transport, make sure that it's properly maintained. Check tyres, brakes, oil and lights a few days before the competition. Make sure that you've got proper horse transport breakdown recovery in place just in case. If you're travelling with a friend they will need to do the same.

Professional transport can be a bit of a minefield with so many people to choose from at so many different prices. Make some enquiries and find a transporter that your friends trust or that you've used yourself and been pleased with. You want your horse to have a good journey so that they can arrive at the venue relaxed and ready to work. Make sure that your transporter is properly licensed and insured.

On the day, be clear in your mind about who is going to be loading and handling your horse. I'm sure in most cases that will be yourself but if you are going to be helped by the transporter make sure that they know that they need to be kind to your horse and handle them sympathetically. You need to know that if your horse gets worried about loading, they won't be rushed and will be treated kindly.

Taking time to plan ahead for competition day will make the whole experience a lot more enjoyable.

What to bring to a competition

For the horse

- Food
- Water
- Hay
- Saddle and bridle
- First aid kit
- Whip
- Grooming kit and cleaning products
- Horse treats (apples or carrots)
- Leg / travel bandages
- Talk bandage

For the human

- Drink, lunch, snacks
- Riding clothes and jacket

- Riding boots and chaps
- Riding hat
- Spare clothes if you get wet
- Copy of the dressage test
- Spurs if needed
- Cleaning products for you
- Safety pins for numbers
- Gloves (do not forget these!)
- Hairnet
- Tie or stock
- Your lucky charm if you have one!
- Food or snacks to keep your energy levels up
- Sunscreen
- First aid kit

Tip: Organise everything in your car the night before. Invest in some boxes and bags and put similar items together so they are easy to find when you are at the competition.

The week before

If you haven't been to a venue before, visit it a few days before to see what it's like and how it's laid out, or use Google or Facebook to see what the facilities are like. Is the arena beside a busy restaurant? Is there a train line nearby? How far away is the parking from the arena? Then you can focus more on your test and your horse, not on navigating your way to the venue and wondering what you'll find when you arrive.

Your horse is usually at their most relaxed in their home environment. You've probably heard people say 'but they're not like this at home' about their horse! It is very useful training to take your horse somewhere else – perhaps a friend's place or a local stables, and ride your dressage test there as practise in an unfamiliar place. It's a dry run for the official day, and also a good way to see if you can remember your test when under pressure in a new place!

Also practise loading your horse into a trailer.

You could also invite a friend to come with you! It's lovely to have an extra pair of hands on the day to help you out, and give you moral support.

The night before

- Check the air pressure on all tyres, including the spare.
- Make sure the wheels are on OK and the wheel nuts are tight.
- Clean windows, windscreen and mirrors and fill up screen wash.
- Check your trailer and car have both oil and water.
- Connect the trailer to the car and check all indicators are working.
- Do an overall visual inspection, making sure there are no signs of oil or fuel leaks.
- Pack your car with as much as you can.
- Have a water container and bucket on board in case your horse needs a drink if you get delayed.
- Print out your test and put it in the car.
- Put details of your insurance and breakdown recovery in the vehicle.
- Write up a 'to do' list on your phone to make sure you don't forget anything.
- Put some snacks and a drink in your car.
- Put sunscreen and a waterproof coat in your car, along with a change of clothing for if you get wet.
- Invite a friend. It can be really handy to bring a friend who can hold your horse while you go to the bathroom, call out the test if required and be an extra pair of hands for you.
- Check the directions for your event.

- Check you have enough gas or petrol in your car.
- Read through the event rules one more time.
- Pack as much as possible. Make sure everything is clean.

One more important thing to do to make sure your transport, whether a lorry or trailer, is in good repair – check the floor and ramp regularly. Make sure they are cleaned properly after every trip but be aware that drainage might not be particularly efficient and wooden floors can rot, so have a look before every trip.

How to approach your first few dressage test days

Think of using your first few competitions as part of your training program. Just by getting there on the day you've done so much already! This is a great way to take all the pressure off yourself and your horse. It doesn't matter if you get top of the score sheet or bottom. You've done a ton of work to make it to this day and you and your horse are already winners in my eyes.

Having help from a caller

In most instances in affiliated dressage, you can have a caller at the side of the arena for support. They will have a copy of the dressage test and can call out instructions to you to help you to ride the test accurately. They can't coach you but they can pre-warn you about the '20 metre circle at A'. When you've got a couple of competitions under your belt you probably won't need this and will memorise the tests, but when you're getting started it's a great help and confidence boost. If you have an experienced friend who could do this for you it's worth considering.

Prepare yourself mentally as well. Don't put yourself under too much pressure, you need to enjoy yourself. Think of it as just another day out enjoying riding your horse.

The people you meet at competitions

You'll meet all sorts at competitions, let's face it, us horsey people can be an interesting bunch! Potentially though, a competition can be an opportunity to meet new contacts and future dressage buddies. I'd say be ready to steer clear if need be, but helpful and friendly when you can. These are the sort of things people might appreciate help with:

- Holding their horse while they grab a snack or go to the bathroom.
- Producing a handy bit of baling twine to sort out any number of emergencies.
- Offering to call their test.
- Finding a safety pin for their numbers.
- Just having a friendly chat if they look nervous.

Advice from judges

All judges have different feedback approaches. Some are very honest, maybe more honest than some of us would like! However, many riders appreciate getting a 'warts and all' style feedback, as it's clear to understand. But some riders can take this criticism to heart and get quite upset. Some judges are wonderfully kind and tactful. Whatever style your judge happens to have, remember – they might have a different standard to you, or they might not value the same things in the test.

The judge might value different aspects of your riding and how your horse is working to you. They might overlook something you were thrilled about. They might find fault with something that you didn't even notice.

It's not worth crying over. Your true judge is your horse. If your horse is happy and healthy, then you're doing a great job. It doesn't matter what a judge you don't know says!

If you think about it, going to a show and allowing a stranger to judge us and our horse in just 3 – 4 minutes - someone we've never met, we have no idea of their riding ethos or skills and they are going to judge when us when we are under pressure and in a new environment - it's a weird and brave thing to do!

The big day

Allow extra time to get to the competition venue, as time goes quickly once you arrive and register. You might have to fix a few plaits. You might need to change a flat tire. You might meet a friend and realise you're running late. So give yourself lots of time in your schedule. What would normally take 15 minutes will take 30 minutes on test day. So be very generous with your time. It's better to be early than to be late! It's a good idea to wear tracksuit bottoms and a sweater/jumper over your dressage clothes from early morning, to stop them getting dirty before your test begins.

Arrival at the venue

Spend ten minutes or more walking your horse in hand around the venue. I would do this in a halter with a 12 foot rope. This will help your horse to relax and get used to the new place and having so many other horses around. It is an effective way to reduce unwanted tension in your horse's body, allow their mind to settle and prepare them to be ridden in the warm up arena. It also allows your horse to stretch their legs and begin to slowly warm up their muscles after their trip in the trailer, reducing the risk of injury when you ride. An added bonus – it will help you to relax too!

Allow your horse to investigate new things. If they see something that makes them nervous, let them take their time, allow them to stop and look for 10-20-30 seconds - as long as they need to. It could be something as simple as a flower pot, or as understandable as the beer tent. You stand between your horse and the worrying object at first, then step to one side when you feel them relax a bit. The philosophy is to allow your horse the time they need to look at the object from all angles and when they are ready, be 100% fine with it. This exercise not only solves the issues of the scary object in question, but actually builds your horse's overall confidence in new places, and their trust in you. This is all critical because when you're in the arena there will be more random flower pots, activity from spectators, strange buildings and tents to contend with. Not to mention the judges – often sat at one end peering through a car windscreen. It's pretty common when you're at a competition venue to see a rider dealing with a horse that's really worried and bouncing all over the place. Often there will be several people trying to help them, which to be honest can help or hinder! Nobody wants to leave the arena on a scared horse after say a bit of a buck then a full-blown run out – and it won't help your marks either!

Tacking up - Instead of doing the girth up fully (in one go) while your horse is standing still, it is more kind/comfortable for the horse to do the girth up in a few stages and ask your horse to walk a little in between stages.

Always be kind to your horse, both in the getting ready, warmup and during the test. You are being watched so just like at home, support and be kind to your horse.

The warm up arena

Make sure your numbers are on correctly and visible.

Make sure the clerk knows you are there.

Identify any horse that looks unsettled or problematic and stay away from them.

Follow the rules of the warmup area. For example, passing with your left side to the left of other riders is the correct etiquette in many countries, often referred to as 'left to left'. Check with the steward or ask a local rider outside the warmup ring what is expected of you, if you aren't certain.

If any horse gets loose in the arena, follow that horse at the walk at a sensible distance. If you are following a loose horse, they are less unlikely to run straight into you. When you let your horse look at trouble you help them to feel calmer and let them see what is going on. This keeps both of you safer.

Arenas can be busy areas. This means that you need to keep your eyes open and wits about you just in case another rider who isn't concentrating rides across your line. Getting put off course is frustrating at the walk, but much more so at the canter. Hopefully the warm up arena is well managed so that there are not too many horses in it at once, which really helps.

If your horse has a bit more energy in the warm up arena than you would like, work first on exercises that ask them to concentrate a bit, such as small circles, small serpentines and lateral work. Don't transition up out of the walk until your horse is with you.

If your horse lacks energy in the warmup arena, work on larger circles and straight lines, which will encourage them to think forward.

Ideally, after you warm up, you will not be standing still for a long time waiting for your test to begin.

Ride in the warm up arena how you plan to ride in the test. It doesn't matter what other riders are doing, remember how you and your horse work together when you are feeling secure at home and carry on in that way. Sometimes there is some pretty horrible riding in warm ups. You might see people holding their horses in hyperflexion, practising the Rollkur method. Nothing justifies putting a horse under such pressure at any time, even if it does sometimes appear to be rewarded in the judging. Avoid that path at all costs, remember that you listen to your horse.

About the warm up process

A warm up process is necessary to reduce and prevent strains and injury for your horse. Many horses will have travelled and may be a little stiff from the trailer. The warm up allows their muscles to relax, their bodies to supple up, and gets them ready to give their best in the arena without risking injury.

Begin with a forwards walk on a loose rein. Allow your horse to stretch out his muscles. Think forwards and relaxed, and use the exercises that your horse needs at the time, as mentioned above. When your horse feels ready, add in some transitions.

When trotting, try rising trot to allow your horse to move his back and continue to warm up.

As you warm up, take note of any resistance you feel in your horse's body. Do they feel a little lame? Are they a little stiff? Are they bending and softening better on one side than the other?

Be aware of anything like this as you work and if your horse seems uncomfortable or not loose enough to work hard, consider whether you want to carry on to do the test.

Focus on having a nice relaxed, forward moving horse working with a good rhythm.

As the warm up continues, ask your horse for a little collection, for them to start to transfer some weight from the forequarter to the hind quarters. You can include any of the collection riding exercises earlier on in this book.

How to remember your test

Remember, if you have trouble memorising your test, or are worried that you might forget it in the heat of the moment, you can always use a caller.

- Practice drawing the test out on paper.
- Record the test on your phone and listen while you ride.
- Walk the test around your kitchen every evening.
- Write the test up from memory.
- Walk the steps yourself in the arena.

Seriously though - practice, but not so much that your horse gets drilled. If that happens they might either start to anticipate the movements and do things before you ask, or they can start to switch off completely. If you need to keep repeating the patterns to fix them in your mind – as above, walk it through yourself. Great exercise!

Managing competition nerves

The best way to manage competition nerves is to start by avoiding competitions until you've got some practise in and confidence developed at home. Then gradually work from small, informal venues to the busier and fancier places.

Start by competing at home, by doing and videoing an online dressage test. There are various online shows out there, and you'll get the practise of doing a test and getting tips and feedback from the judge.

Ask a few friends to come along and watch you ride your test. If they are horsey friends you can invite constructive feedback, or decide that you'd rather they didn't, it's up to you.

Use a lesson with your trainer to ride your test just as if you were at a show and ask them to mark it and give you feedback.

Start with a few low-level showing events for a low stress way to find your feet.

Remember which way you need to turn when you enter the arena at A. If you keep that in mind as you approach it will help the rest of your test click into place.

Just think of the judge as another trainer working with you and giving you suggestions/things to work on. That is the point of 'showing' dressage. It helps you know how you're doing and how you can improve. Try not to think of it as a test or a competition.

Dressage is a learning journey. It is a partnership between you and your horse. You are competing ONLY against your last test score, or maybe to improve the most recent movements that you are trying to get down. Your competition does not matter. Enjoy the ride.

Remember – 'I am here to have fun. My life is not in danger and I am choosing to be here.' And smile! It puts you at ease.

A lot of riders find that Bach's Rescue Remedy helps to calm their nerves, so bear that in mind.

Take someone with you to the event that can help you with your horse and talk to you before you go in.

Don't look at it as a competition, look at it as training. And remember, if it goes badly, it doesn't matter! As long as you're out there having a good time with your horse. Nothing else matters. Also, if you forget the test or if the horse acts up, I promise you nobody is looking going 'OMG look at her!', they'll look and think 'We've all been there, I feel for her.' Have fun and enjoy being with your horse, that's the main thing.

Sing or hum a song that's easy to remember to yourself. It's a super way to distract yourself from the anxiety! Your horse will feel your muscles relax as well!

Competition tips

Walk around outside the arena when you're called in to help your horse feel comfortable, be friendly and greet the judges.

Do not start your test until given the go ahead. If there is room, start your centreline before you enter the arena.

When you are saluting the judge, carry your whip in the hand that does not salute.

Breathe while you are riding. I'm not joking ☺

Have fun! Dressage can become very serious, especially if you're dedicated. It's an exacting discipline which, if taken too seriously, can zap all the fun out of riding. Lighten up, soften up and laugh! Once I started to laugh at my failings and mistakes, instead of getting mad and aggressive at myself, my riding changed... and so did my horse! We've been having fun together ever since.

If your horse doesn't feel right in the warm up or during any part of the test... don't risk injury and consider withdrawing. Injuries can take a long time to heal, and 5 minutes of doing just that one test could result in 4-8 weeks of missing training and tests in the future. Health comes first always.

After your test

Walk your horse after your test to allow them to cool down. This prevents injury and muscle stiffness.

No matter how well your test went, be sure to praise your horse and thank them for their efforts. They didn't ask to be put into a trailer, drive for miles and made to ride around a sand arena in a strange place! Always be grateful.

Your test results

Just a final think about judges and results, it bears repeating! Some judges will dish out critical comments unvarnished and to the point. Others will be kinder, and phrase their comments in a way that will help us to develop our dressage. We might look back on the test and think 'Yes, that's a fair comment.' or we might cry 'Were they looking at the same test?? Have they mixed us up with another horse and rider?'. If it's useful constructive criticism, learn from it, if it's not helpful forget it!

Common dressage questions and issues

Here are some common questions and challenges that dressage riders have.

My horse is slowing down when doing lateral work

There are two useful strategies to try. First, half way through your lateral movement, ask your horse to change gait upwards. So you can start a leg yield in walk, and half way through the leg yield start trotting.

A second method is to complete the leg yield in walk, but always move up one gait the moment the movement is over.

My trainer tells me my leg position is incorrect

You can't keep your legs steady, or your instructor tells you your legs are too far back or too far forward.

The situation is that the saddle you use has a tremendous influence on your position in the saddle. You will often find that you can change your position in the saddle from 'not great' to 'amazing' in two seconds by sitting in a different saddle.

You should not need to always be fighting to hold your legs in a position that doesn't feel natural as you ride. Firstly, it's a good way to tire yourself out. Secondly, holding this tension in your legs will not benefit your horse's way of moving. Consider whether, although your saddle might fit your horse, it might not be quite right for you. See if you can try some different saddles. Try them out and then look at them to identify why they feel different. Look at the differences in design, the stirrup bars may be in different places, you might not be sitting in the lowest part of the seat or your legs might be fixed by the design. Your tack should work for you and your horse - not against you both.

My horse tosses or shakes his head when I ride

The judge might say that your horse is very fussy with their head, and deducts some marks in your test. Your horse gets regular physios, had a comprehensive vet check, saddle check, etc and you've tried changing bits but nothing worked.

One thing I would suggest as an experiment is to borrow a bitless bridle - a simple sidepull, and not a hackamore (which has extra leverage) - and find somewhere safe to ride. Ride in the sidepull in walk and trot for 5-10 minutes. Your horse's response will quickly rule out whether or not this is a bit issue.

My horse rushes or is too fast.

Horses can rush forwards to get away from pain. Ask a physio to check your horse's body and back for pain. Ask a dentist to visit and look for any damage inside your horses from the bit. A bit used by hard hands, or one that doesn't fit, can cause tongue damage or discolouration, bruising on the bars of the both, damage to the roof of mouth and other issues. Also look for general teeth issues like sharp teeth and any mouth ulcers. Alternatively, your horse may be rushing just because they are anticipating the next move. In that case refer back to the exercises in the book and work on simple transitions, halt and backup etc, to help them to think differently.

My horse's canter seems uncoordinated and not very smooth

You are finding it hard to canter for too long without your horse going back to trot.

Check that your horse is breathing when they canter. Listen or ask someone watching to listen. You should be able to hear your horse breathe out per canter stride. Start to notice when your horse holds their breath. Do they also do it in trot? Is it in specific movements? Or in a certain location? Are you holding your breath too?

Consider also calling an equine physiotherapist to work on your horse, relax the muscles that may be tight, which should also benefit your horse.

I need help to get my horse on the bit!

Your horse does it sometimes, but not others. Sometimes it happens when you are using a gadget like a chambon or something else along those lines. But you want it to be from your aids and to be consistent. What should you do?

Throw away the chambon. Just encourage your horse to move forward with energy. Honestly it will come with time. Go back to basics and work through the collection exercises in this book. When your horse starts to understand how to shift their weight to their hind end, collection will start to follow. Horses need to learn how to collect and carry themselves, and to find that collection is a safe place.

What dressage saddle design is best?

Why do some dressage saddles have higher pommels, cantles and bigger knee blocks than others? And which is best?

Bigger blocks mean that it's easier to 'lock' into a position- making it easier to sit the bigger gaits of modern dressage horses. The bad thing about that is it means we stop moving, meaning the horse's back stops moving. Sometimes these types of saddles are trying to make up for lack of time spent developing a seat by fixing the rider in one (problematic?) posture. When the rider is fixed in one position they almost always end up behind the motion of their horse.

There is a theory that these saddles that fix the rider firmly became fashionable around the same time as Rollkur. They certainly make it easier for the rider to brace and have more leverage against the horse.

The older saddles have a larger weight bearing surface, meaning that the rider sits closer to the horse. This allows the rider to have an independent seat – they are freer to position the entire leg and stay over the centre of motion.

If the rider is able to ride with more freedom, their instructor will get a truer picture of their strengths and weaknesses and it will be easier to help them with their position.

My horse leans on my hands. How do I fix this?

Let's look at what this feels like. It might feel like your shoulders are being pulled out of their sockets. Or that there's a block of concrete at the end of your reins, pulling very hard on your hands. A horse should never be allowed to lean on your hands. It means they are unbalanced and on the forehand. This leaning also makes it incredibly difficult for the rider to successfully complete any dressage manoeuvres or think of beginning collection.

Apart from the fact that if a horse is leaning heavily on their rider's hands it is not healthy for them, it is also not pleasant for their rider.

Here is how to fix it. Sit tall in your saddle with your head up and looking forward. Ask your horse for a soft contact, then breathe in, sit tall and ask them to move forward. If your horse is in the habit of leaning on your hands you will probably feel them start to do that almost immediately. As soon as you feel it, close your fingers on the reins, think backward and ask your horse to do between 1-3 steps backward. Go back as many steps as you need to until you feel your horse soften and take their weight off your hands. Don't make this into a fight, if you start pulling they will push against you. Think in terms of you being a fence post, you won't pull back, but you will not give way if you are pulled on. Let your horse pause to think, before asking them to soften and walk off again. Be consistent; practise this as many times as you need to for your horse to change their mind about pushing forward into your hands.

It's fine at the beginning if all you get is 1 step forwards without pushing! That's not uncommon when working on this issue. With this exercise we can only accept steps forwards with lightness. If they are heavy, we will back up a few steps instead.

My horse is reluctant to move forward with energy

Every ride this feels like an argument. You start off with a light cue for forward, but as you don't get the response you want, you end up escalating to 'pony club kicking'.

First check that there is nothing physical making your horse reluctant to move:

- Get your horse checked physically by a physio
- Ask the dentist to check your horse's teeth
- Make sure that the saddle, bridle and bit are well fitted.

Also consider whether your horse is different when you are riding out on the trail/hacking. If this is an arena problem they may just be bored and need a break from schooling.

When you have checked these things work on the problem in the arena. I have learned to be very patient in these circumstances. Potter around at first, then ask for some leg yielding, and transitions from halt to trot. Praise your horse generally and maybe scratch their withers when they respond.

Use the transitions exercises explained earlier in this book.

Some horses are just a bit slower than others, they have more backward than forward in them. There are a lot of riders who would only be too happy to have a horse like that, that they feel safe on, they can be worth their weight in gold!

My horse opens his mouth when I'm riding

This is going to be either down to how your horse's mouth feels, or how your hands feel. First of all check how the bit fits, ideally with the help of a bit fitter or dentist. Check for:

- Rounded or sharp bars
- Thick or thin tongue, wide or narrow tongue,
- Low or high palette.
- A tooth in the way where the bit should lie
- Ulcers or injury in the mouth.

When you have reassured yourself that the bit is sitting comfortably in your horse's mouth, check out your riding. As your horse is opening their mouth in downward transitions – how are you asking for them? Be aware if you are making sudden movements and snatching the rein. Are you remembering to ask from your body before taking up the rein?

Should I use more leg pressure?

Your instructor tells you to use more leg pressure when you ride your horse.

When your instructor rides your horse, he rides your horse into a firm contact, holding their head into the contact, using a lot of leg pressure. You feel that you need to learn to do the same.

But here's the issue. No rider should need to use a lot of leg pressure (or rein pressure) to ask a horse to either collect (a change in balance, with a little weight transferring from fore to hind legs), or to move forwards with more energy. If you ride your horse in a firm contact, and push them forward hard from your legs you are giving conflicting stop/go signals.

You don't need a firm contact to find collection. Collection is developed using lateral work, starting with shoulder in and out.

A lack of energy in a horse could mean a few things, but a more holistic approach would be advised - first check their diet matches their level of work. In terms of your instructor riding your horse into a ball - this is not the goal of dressage.

Your horse's nose should be vertical or ahead of the vertical, and never behind the vertical or tucked into his

chest. Your horse's poll (the area between their ears) should be the highest point of their body.

If your horse has his nose behind the vertical line a lot when your instructor rides him, you probably need to find another trainer. Your current trainer is using too much force and doesn't understand collection starts from the hindquarters.

Also be aware of posture – yours or your instructor's. If your instructor rides like that they will teach you to do the same. We riders should be sitting tall. There shouldn't be any need to lean back. Apart from the fact that it puts you behind the movement, it also is a clue that the rider is putting a lot of pressure on the horse's mouth. It doesn't help any horse to move freely. This is not a technique I would recommend and I can only imagine how that rein pressure feels on the horse's sensitive mouth!

I've talked about hyperflexion and Rollkur several times. It is physically damaging for horses and the position that they are held in limits their range of sight.

Can I ride bitless?

I'm curious about riding my horse bitless. How would I start?

Well, fortunately I have a bitless book that will help you with this. It sets out the various bitless options available and gives advice on how to get started riding bitless. You can find it here: www.writtenbyelaine.com

What about training young horses?

From time to time I get asked to give advice on problems that people are having when riding young horses, as young as 3 and 4 years old. I really only have one piece of advice to give – the horse is too young for this work. They need to finish fusing their bones and developing their young bodies before we start working them under saddle. As I've mentioned earlier in the book, the human needs to stay on the ground and help their baby horse to prepare for later life with groundwork exercises, keeping it gentle.

Mistakes and problems to avoid

Your hands

- Riding with your hands low and wide will put unwanted pressure on the sensitive bars of the mouth.
- Don't be busy with your hand trying to force a head position, instead work on different manoeuvres, use your legs and seat and the right exercises for collection.
- You should not ride with a fixed hand position. Because your horse's head moves all the time, your hands need to move with your horse's head movement also. So give with your hands at every stride.
- Try not to get your balance from the reins. This doesn't do your horse any good.
- Do not pull the bit from side to side to ask your horse for a particular head-set. This is known as sawing. We are not after a headset. We are aiming for collection which comes from doing lateral exercises which transfers weight from the forequarters to the hindquarters.
- Do not use training aids, gadgets or gizmos as a substitute for good horsemanship and taking the time needed to train your horse and protect his long term health.

Your legs

- Avoid kicking to go forwards. Instead relax and release the tension in your body, lift your energy and use your legs considerately if they are needed.
- Don't nag all the time with your legs. This will desensitise your horse to your legs, and they will mean nothing.
- Do not use a lot of pressure with your legs squeezing on the horses sides the whole time. This restricts the movement of your horse's barrel. This then results in restricting the movement of their legs.

Your riding approach

- Do not physically force a movement, any movement be it lateral, backwards or forward.
- Do not train a young horse too fast. Remember that their bodies aren't physically mature until they are at least 5.5 years old, and usually between 6-8 years.

Collection

- Don't think that collection comes from the head when in fact it comes from the hindquarters.
- Don't rush for results, or concentrate on 'head-set', 'outline' or 'frame'. You can't fake or force collection. It takes time and patience to improve your horse's posture, build up muscles and help him to carry more weight on his hindquarters.

Mindset

- Don't feel you are not good enough to compete. You're fantastic!
- Don't think that dressage is only about competition and scores. Your most important judge is your horse.
- Don't be impatient with your horse. Or yourself. Take some steps back in training. Try to understand what is not working and why. Get the help of someone more advanced than you and who is not only a good dressage rider, but who also has remarkable horsemanship and horse training skills and is kind to the horse.

- Make sure that you don't move on before the basics are in place. If you realise that you have, stop and go back in the process.
- Never give up just because progress seems slow. Rates of progress will vary during the process, but you will improve!
- Make sure that you enjoy spending time doing dressage with your horse. It's meant to be fun and rewarding for both of you. There should be lots of praise for your horse. You should gain a sense of achievement from training a beautiful riding horse.

Bad luck

Sometimes the recommended local trainer is not actually the right one to learn from. If you have doubts or feel uncomfortable, take a break. Just because someone has more certificates hung up on their wall than you do, it doesn't always make them a better horse person. Follow your gut. Always do what's best for your horse.

Saddle design

If it feels wrong it probably is. Make sure that your saddle is right for you and your horse and doesn't restrict the way either of you move.

It's time to get started!

I hope that this book will help you to use dressage to keep your horse fit and healthy and to keep the work fresh and interesting. If at any time you start to feel the pressure to win, or things start to go wrong, dig this book out and take time to refresh on some basics. Make life easy for you and your horse for a while. Taking some time out to relax and smell some roses will pay back in the long term!

The world of dressage can be an intimidating place – but it doesn't have to be! If you keep your focus on doing the best for you and your horse, if you always listen to your horse, you can have fun!

I wish you the very best of luck in your future dressage adventures.

Resources

Horse books for adults

The Equine Listenology Guide
The Listenology Guide to Bitless Bridles
Ozzie, the Story of a Young Horse
Conversations with the Horse
Horse Anatomy Colouring Book

Horse books for kids

P is for Pony – The ABC Alphabet book for Kids 2+
Listenology for Kids age 7-14
Horse Care, Riding and Training for kids 6-11
Horse Puzzles, Games & Brain Teasers for kids 7-14

Books in the Coral Cove Series for kids

The Riding School Connemara Pony
The Storm and the Connemara Pony
The Surprise Puppy and the Connemara Pony

Books in the Connemara Adventure Series for kids

The Forgotten Horse

The Show Horse

The Mayfield Horse

The Stolen Horse

The Adventure Horse

The Lost Horse

All books by Elaine Heney: www.writtenbyelaine.com

iPhone and Android horse riding apps

Dressage tests: www.dressageheroapp.com

Polework training: www.poleworkapp.com

Horse training tracker: www.rideableapp.com

GPS horse riding tracker: www.horsestridesapp.com

Online courses

Shoulder in and out: www.shoulderouttraining.com

All online riding courses: www.greyponyfilms.com

Walk test

The Kilkenny - from the Dressage Hero app

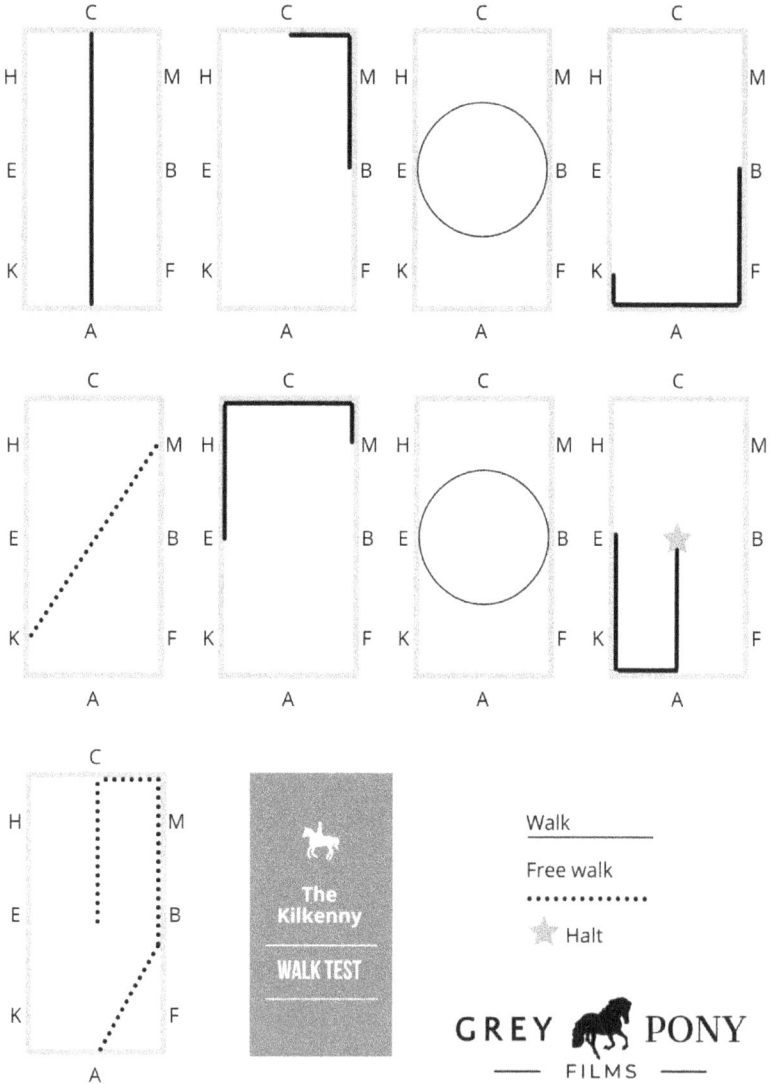

The
Kilkenny

WALK TEST

Walk

Free walk
....

⭐ Halt

GREY PONY
FILMS

AXC: Medium walk

C: Turn right

CMB: Medium walk

B: Circle right 20 metres

BAK: Medium walk

KXM: Free walk on a loose rein

MCHE: Medium walk

E: Circle left 20 metres

EKA: Medium walk

AX: Medium walk

X: Halt, salute

From X, leave arena at A in free walk on a long rein

Trot test

The Sligo - from the Dressage Hero app

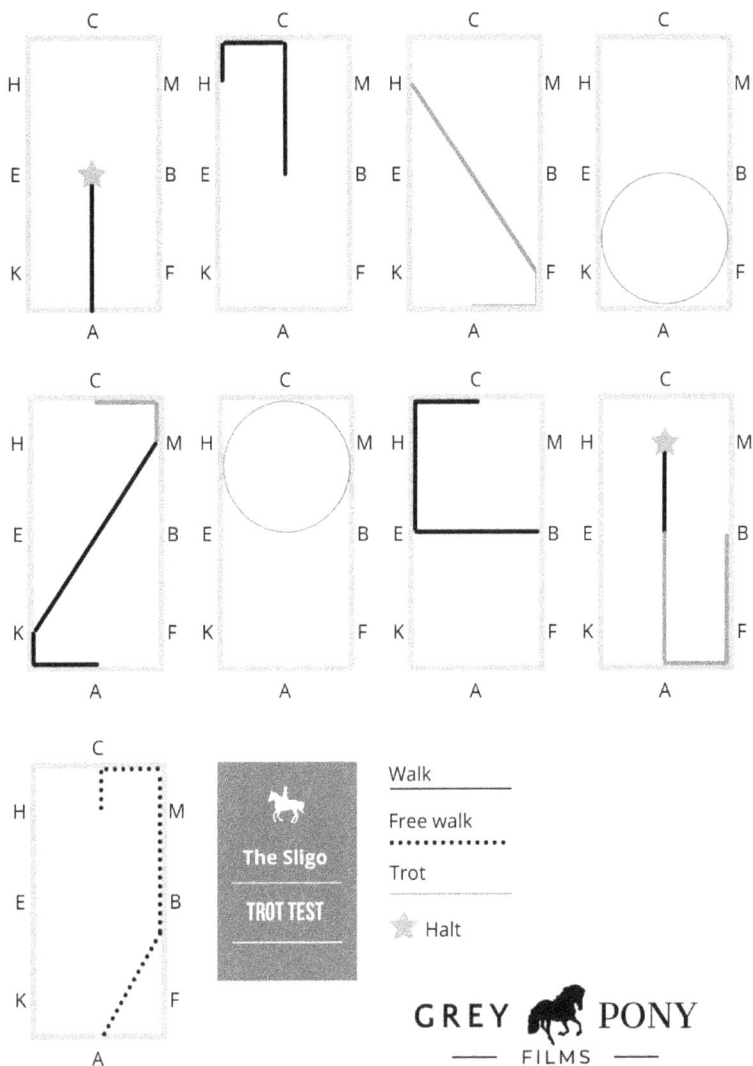

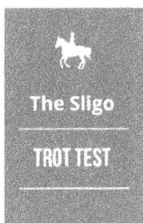

Walk	————
Free walk	··············
Trot	— — — —
⭐ Halt	

The Sligo

TROT TEST

GREY PONY FILMS

COPYRIGHT. NO SHARING PERMITTED.

AX: Medium walk

X: Halt and salute

X to C: Working walk

C: Turn left

CH: Medium walk

HFA: Working trot

A: Circle 20m right, working trot

A: Medium walk

AKM: Medium walk

MC: Working trot

C: Circle 20m left, working trot

C: Medium walk

CEB: Medium walk

BFAX: Working trot

XG: Medium walk

G: Halt, salute

From G, leave arena at A in free walk on a long rein

Canter test

The Meath - from the Dressage Hero app

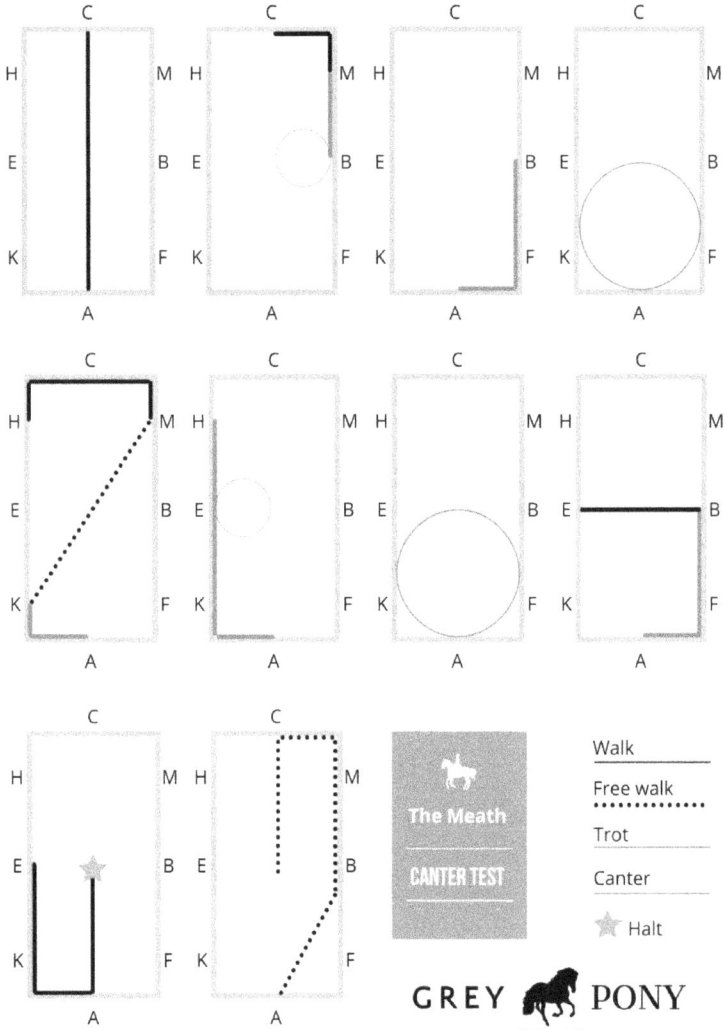

Legend:

Walk ——
Free walk ••••••••
Trot ——
Canter ——
⭐ Halt

GREY PONY FILMS

AXC: Medium walk

C: Turn right

CM: Medium walk

M: Working trot

MB: Working trot

B: Circle right 10m, working trot

BFA: Working trot

A: Circle right 20m, canter

A: Working trot

AK: Working trot

KXM: Free walk on a loose rein

M: Medium walk

MCH: Medium walk

HE: Working trot

E: 10m circle left, working trot

EKA: Working trot

A: 20m circle in canter

A: Working trot

AFB: Working trot

B: Medium walk

BE: Medium walk

EKAX: Medium walk

X: Halt, salute

From X, leave arena at A in free walk on a long rein

Horse books by Elaine Heney

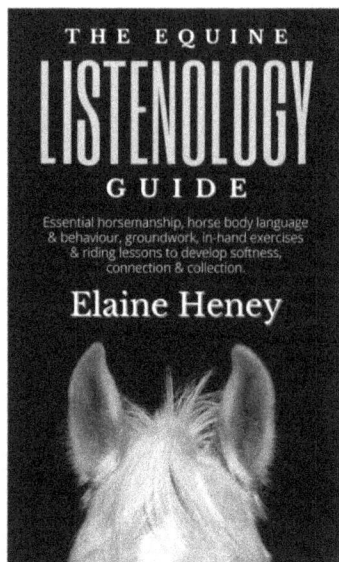

THE EQUINE
LISTENOLOGY
GUIDE

Essential horsemanship, horse body language
& behaviour, groundwork, in-hand exercises
& riding lessons to develop softness,
connection & collection.

Elaine Heney

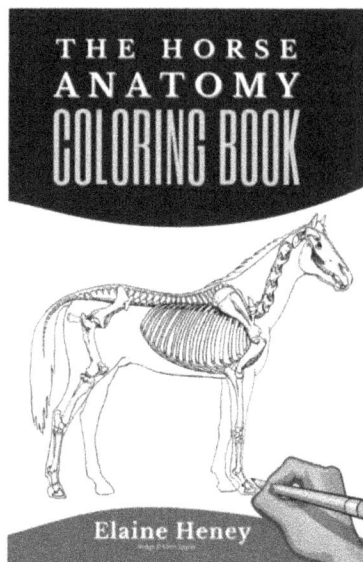

THE HORSE
ANATOMY
COLORING BOOK

Elaine Heney

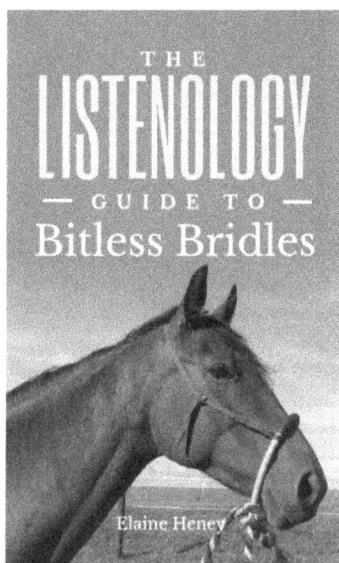

THE
LISTENOLOGY
— GUIDE TO —
Bitless Bridles

Elaine Heney

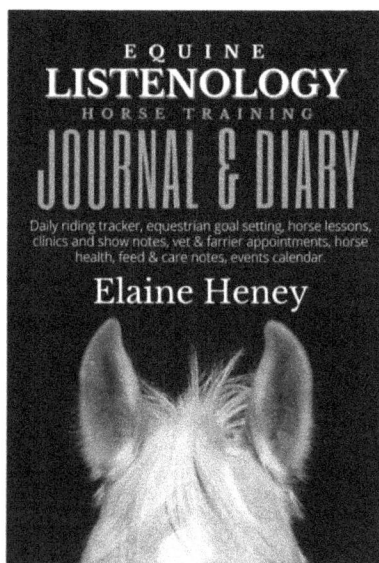

EQUINE
LISTENOLOGY
HORSE TRAINING
JOURNAL & DIARY

Daily riding tracker, equestrian goal setting, horse lessons,
clinics and show notes, vet & farrier appointments, horse
health, feed & care notes, events calendar.

Elaine Heney

EDUCATIONAL HORSE BOOKS FOR KIDS...

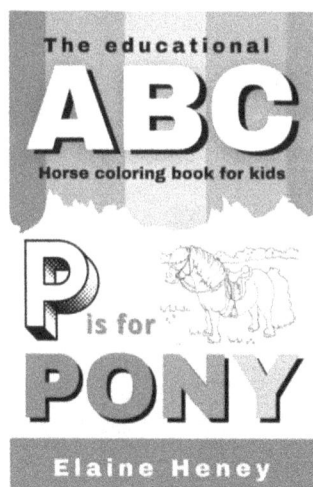

THE
CONNEMARA
ADVENTURE SERIES
FOR KIDS 8+

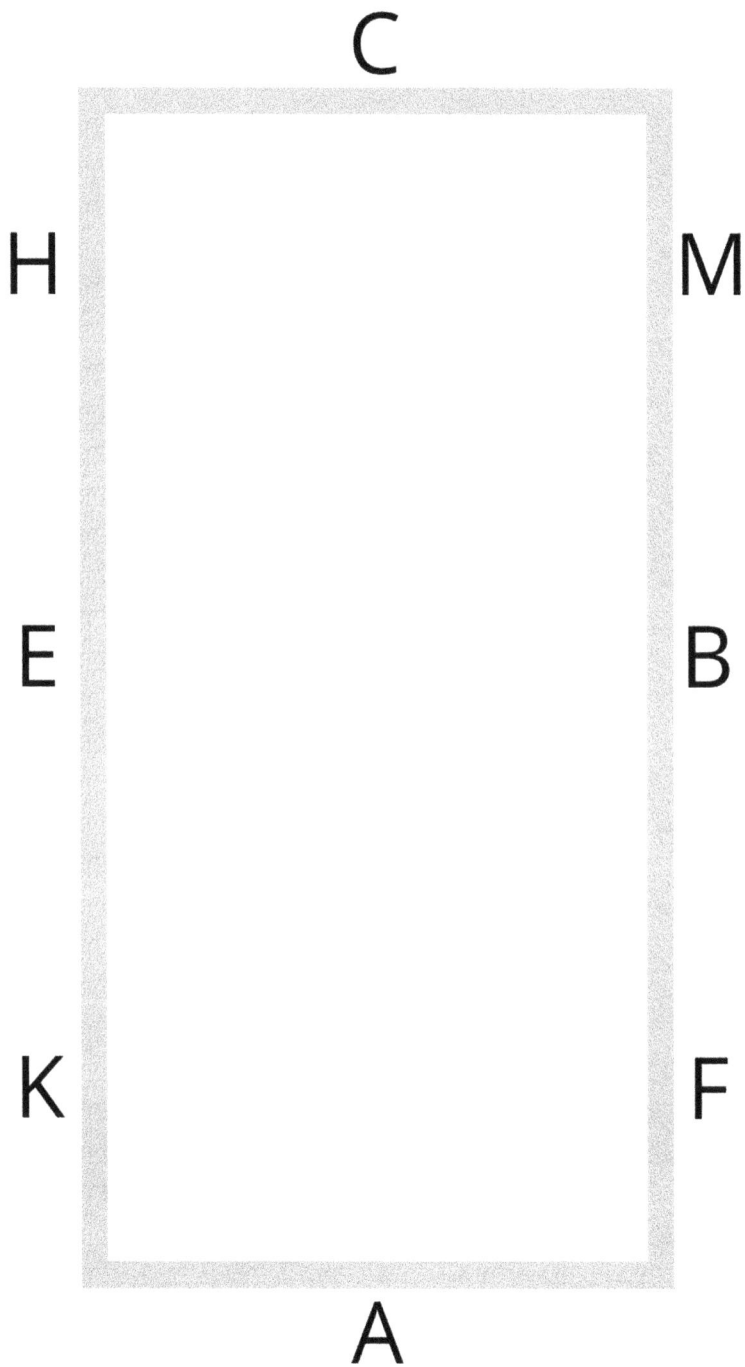

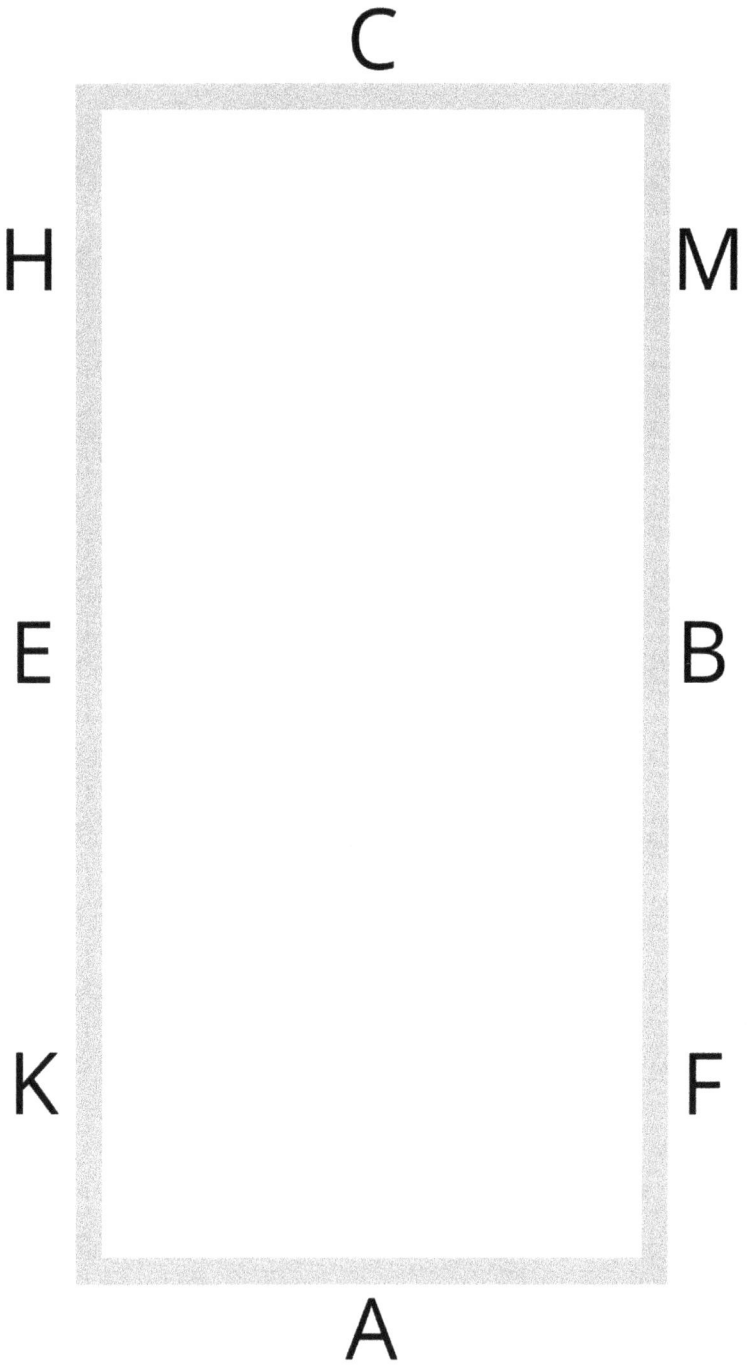

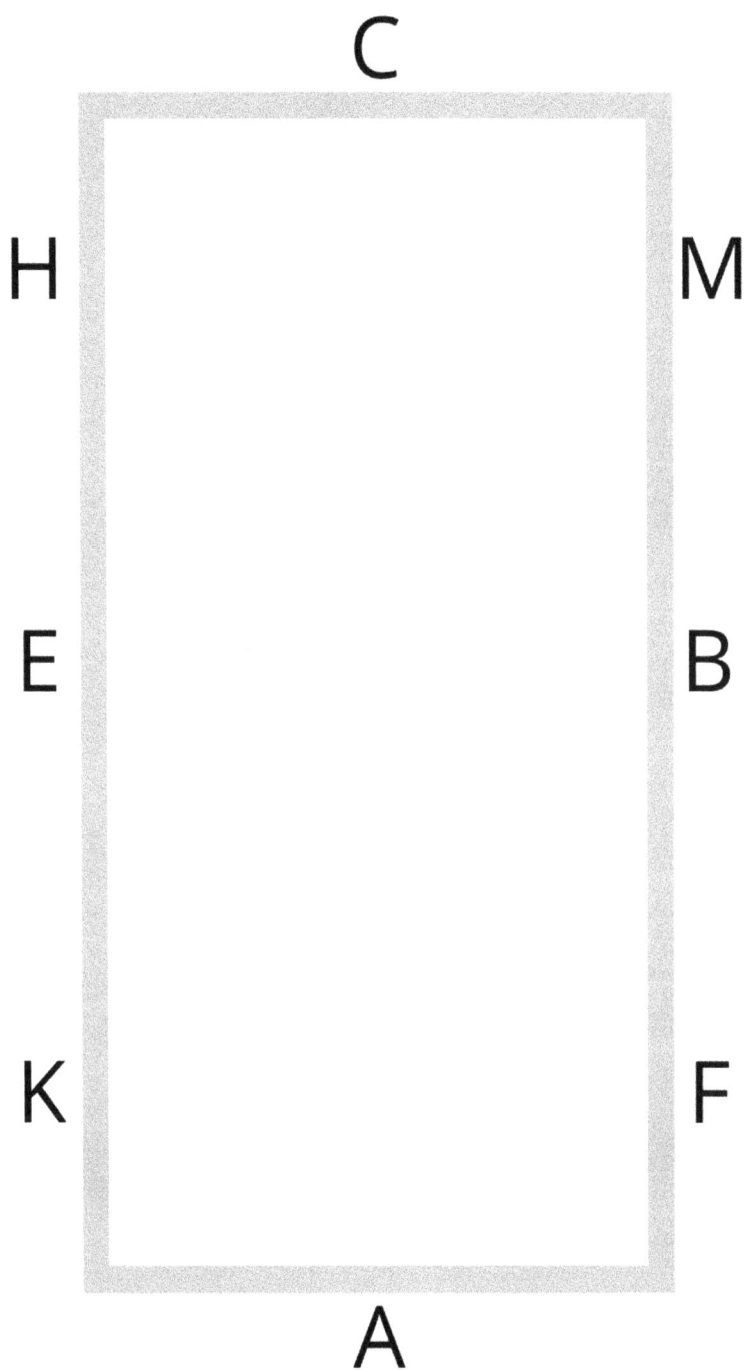

C

H

M

E

B

K

F

A

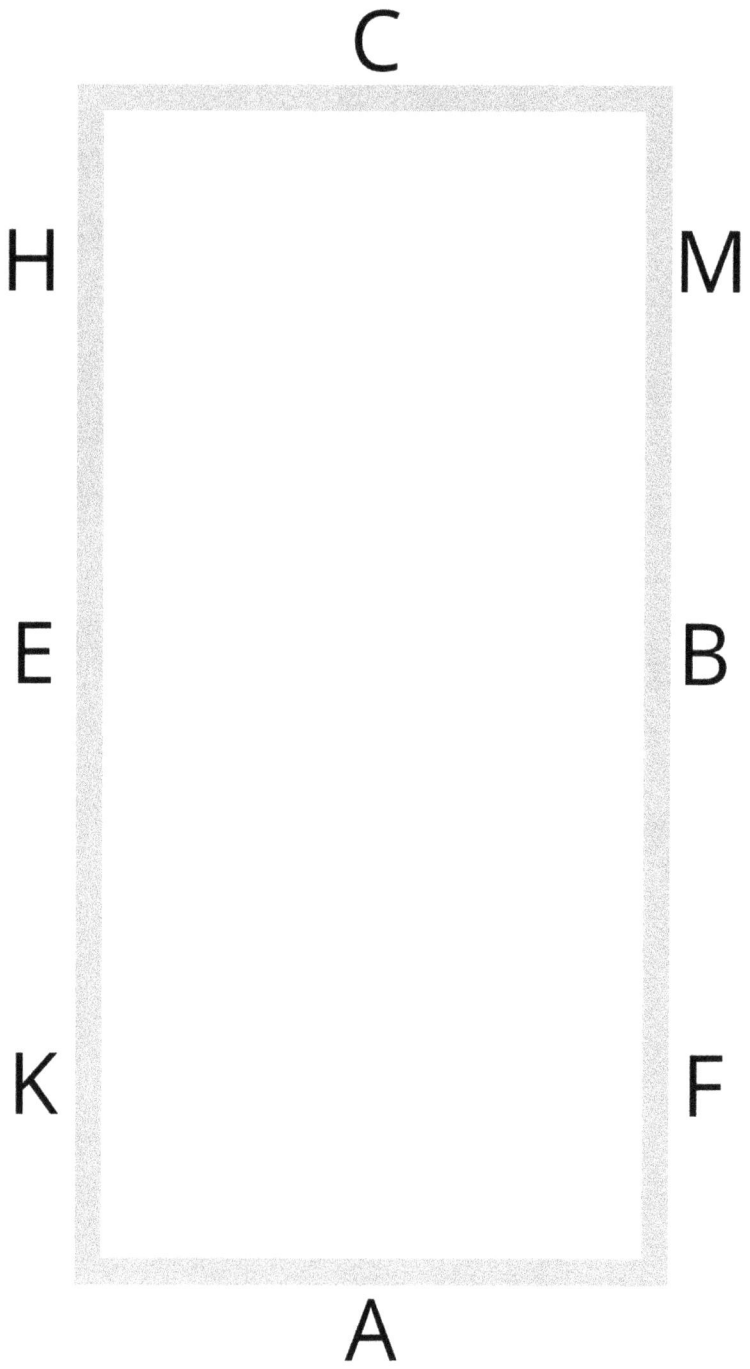

C

H   M

E   B

K   F

A

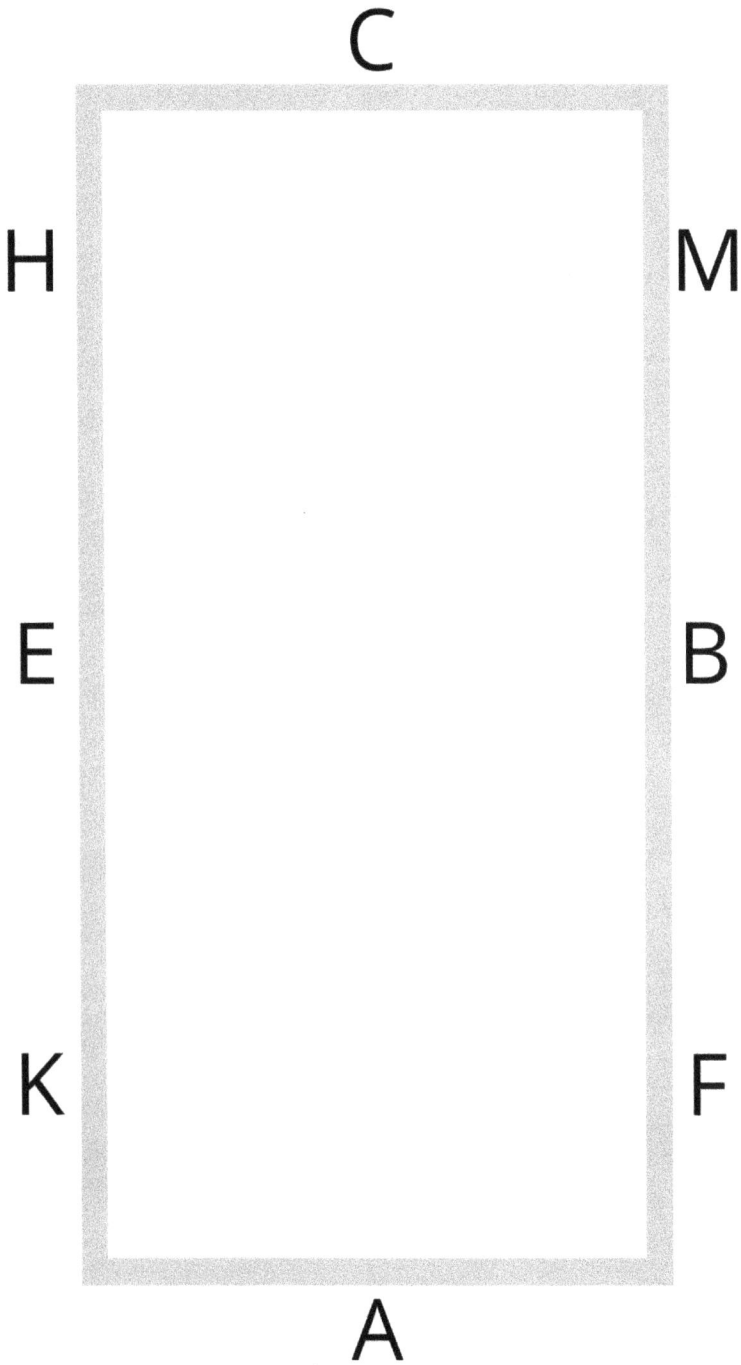

C

H

M

E

B

K

F

A

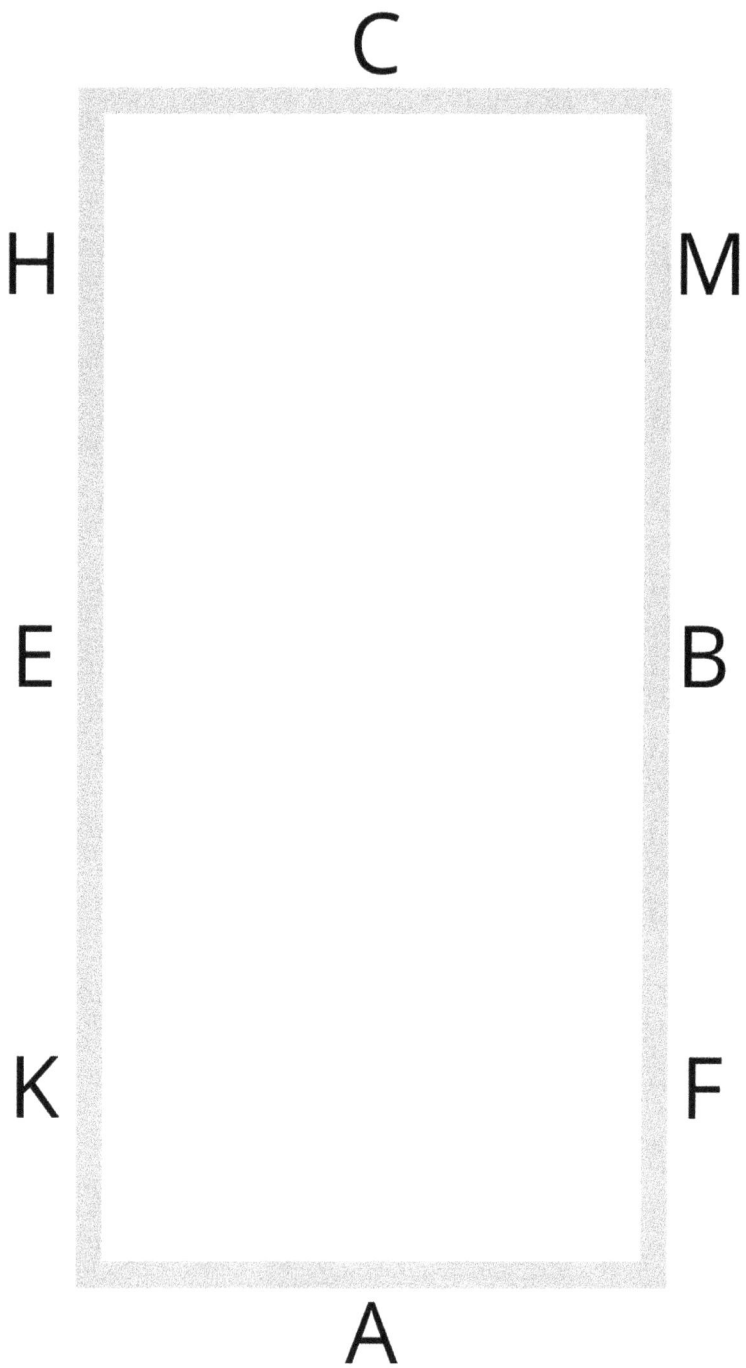

C

H

M

E

B

K

F

A

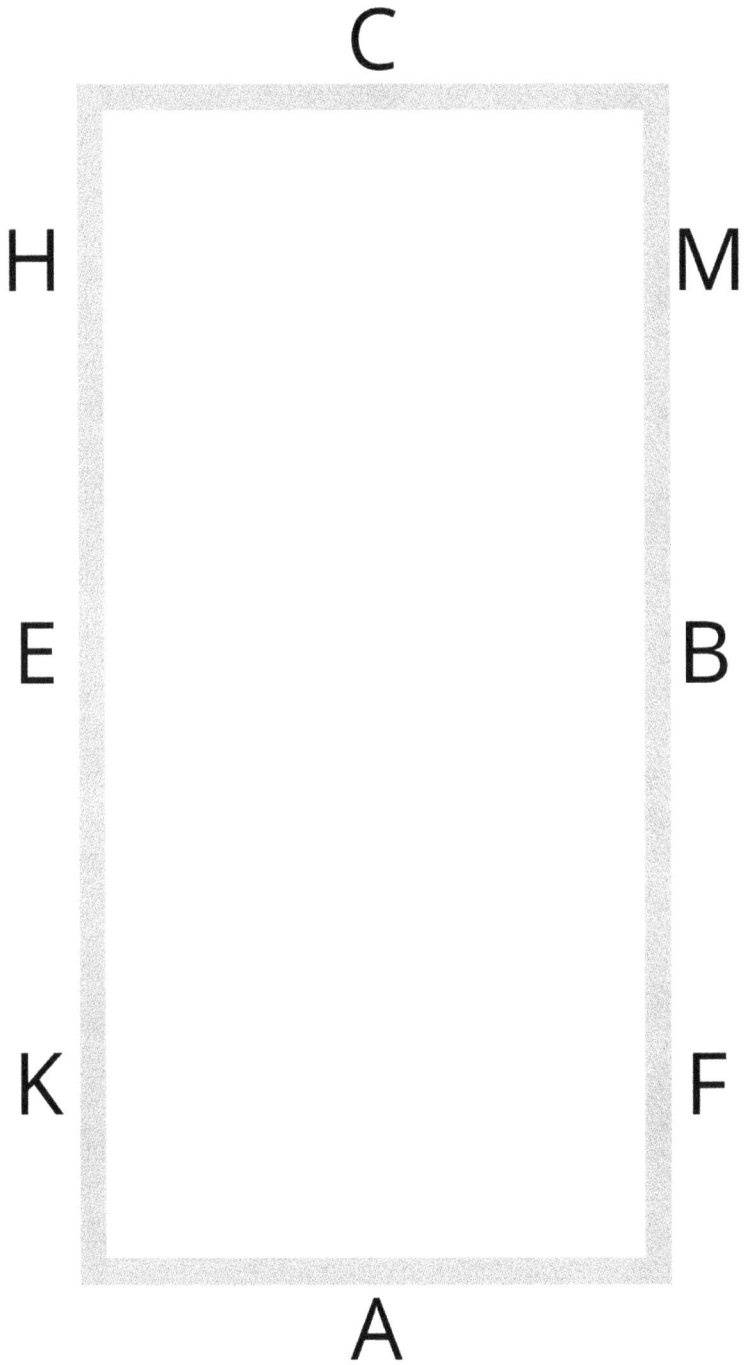

C

H   M

E   B

K   F

A

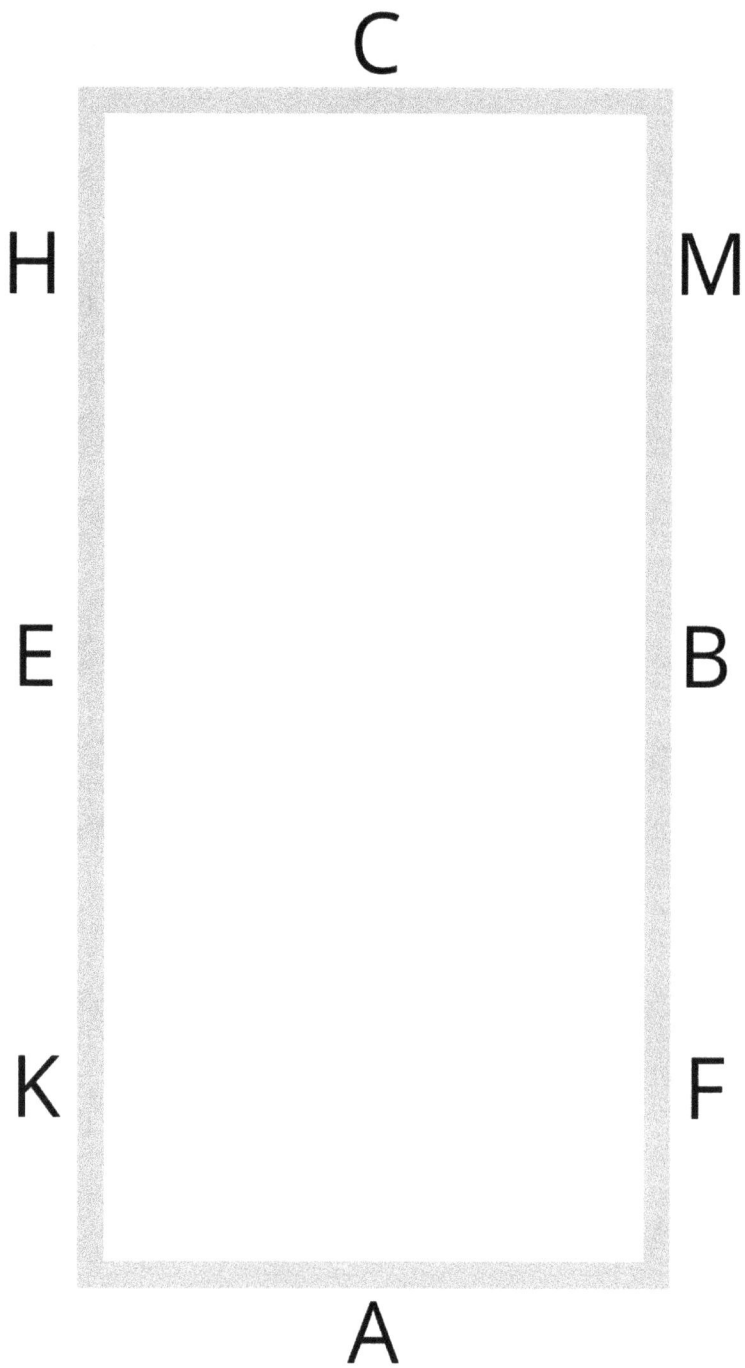

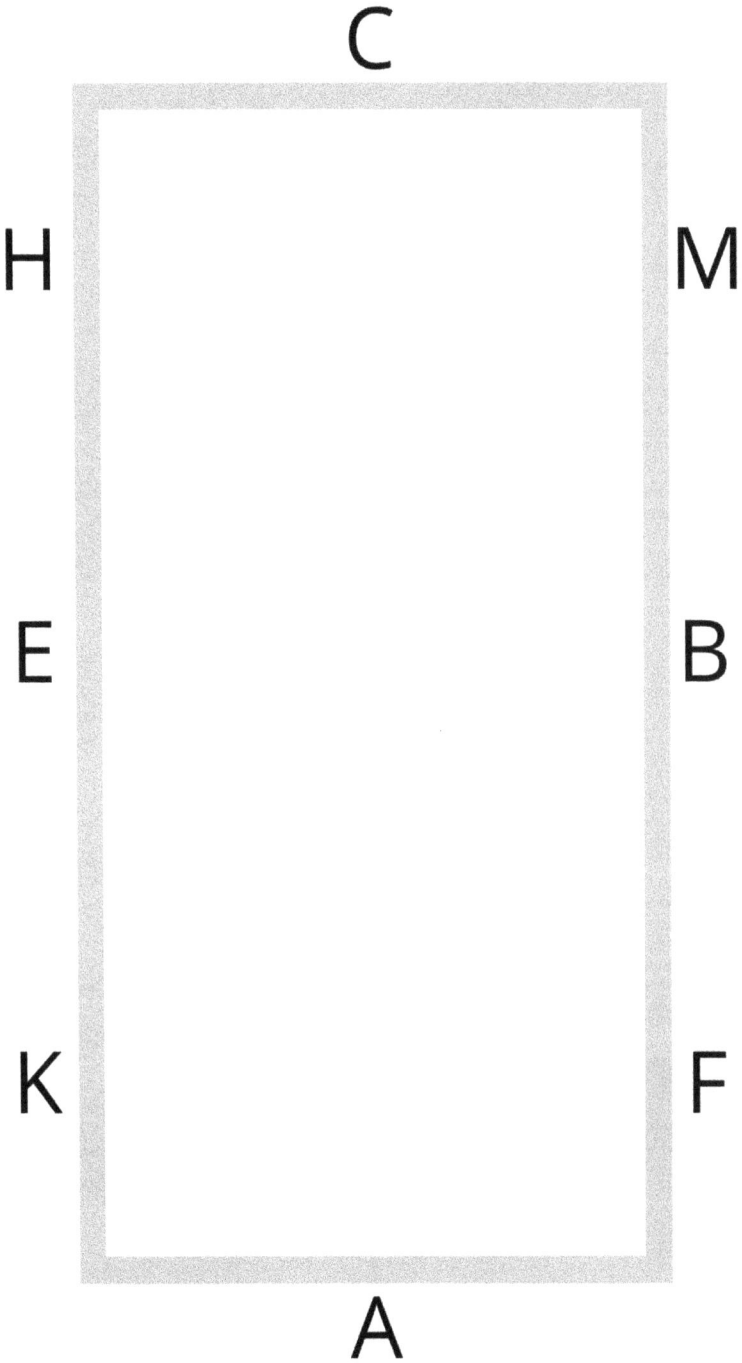

C

H

M

E

B

K

F

A

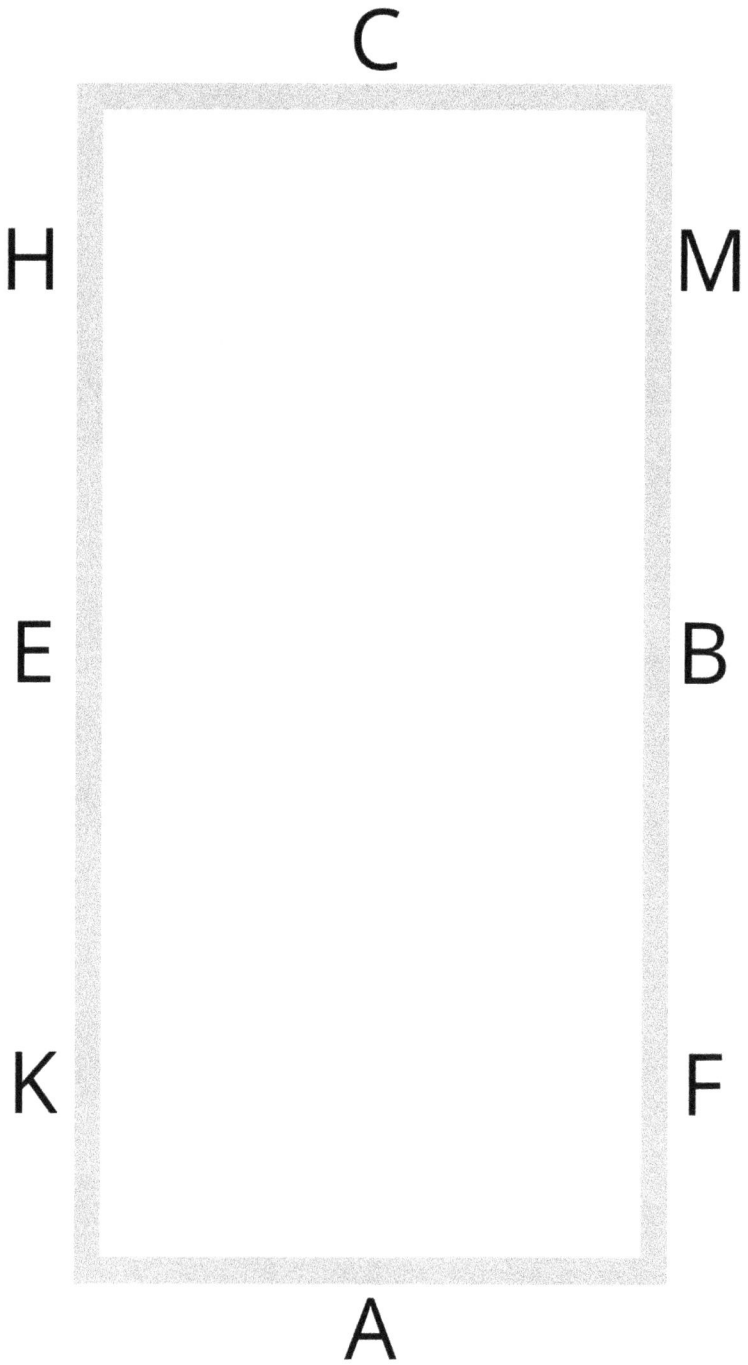

C

H   M

E   B

K   F

A

www.ingramcontent.com/pod-product-compliance
Lightning Source LLC
Chambersburg PA
CBHW050223270326
41914CB00003BA/539